OLD AGE

Recent decades have seen a fundamental change in the age structure of many Western societies. In these societies it is now common for a fifth to a quarter of the population to be retired, for fewer babies to be born than is required to sustain the size of the population and for life expectancy at birth for women to exceed eighty years. This book provides an overview of the key issues arising from this demographic change, asking questions such as:

- What, if any, are the universal characteristics of the ageing experience?
- What different ways is it possible to grow old?
- What is unique about old age in the contemporary world?

The author also examines issues ranging from the social construction, diversity and identity of old age to areas of social conflict over population, pensions and the medicalisation of old age.

John Vincent is Senior Lecturer in Sociology at the University of Exeter.

KEY IDEAS

Series Editor: PETER HAMILTON, The Open University, Milton Keynes

Designed to complement the successful *Key Sociologists*, this series covers the main concepts, issues, debates, and controversies in sociology and the social sciences. The series aims to provide authoritative essays on central topics of social science, such as community, power, work, sexuality, inequality, benefits and ideology, class, family, etc. Books adopt a strong individual 'line' constituting original essays rather than literary surveys, and for lively and original treatments of their subject matter. The books will be useful to students and teachers of sociology, political science, economics, psychology, philosophy and geography.

OLD AGE

John Vincent

Routledge
Taylor & Francis Group

LONDON AND NEW YORK

First published 2003
by Routledge
11 New Fetter Lane, London EC4P 4EE

Simultaneously published in the USA and Canada
by Routledge
29 West 35th Street, New York, NY 10001

Routledge is an imprint of the Taylor & Francis Group

Typeset in Garamond and Scala by Keystroke, Jacaranda Lodge,
Wolverhampton
Printed and bound in Great Britain by
TJ International Ltd, Padstow, Cornwall

British Library Cataloguing in Publication Data
A catalogue record for this book is available from the British Library

Library of Congress Cataloging in Publication Data
Vincent, John A., 1947–
    Old age / John Vincent.
      p. cm. — (Key ideas)
    Includes bibliographical references and index.
    1. Aged—Social conditions. I. Title. II. Series.
    HQ1061 .V541448 2003
    305.26—dc21   2002013053

ISBN 0–415–26822–2 (hbk)
ISBN 0–415–26823–0 (pbk)

For Julie

CONTENTS

ILLUSTRATIONS

FIGURES

TABLES

Acknowledgements

Thanks are due for the help given by Mari Shullaw of Routledge and my daughter Sarah Vincent through their comments on drafts of this book. Two anonymous referees also gave helpful advice which was much appreciated. I have referred to empirical research I have conducted in Ireland, Bosnia and the UK. I wish to gratefully acknowledge the help of all the older people, and others, who helped with that research. In particular, the contributions to those studies by Zeljka Mudrovcic, my co-researcher in Bosnia, and Karen Wale and Guy Patterson who assisted on the research into older people's politics in the UK funded by the Leverhulme Trust. I have used data from data sets supplied by the ESRC Data Archive at the University of Essex, specifically the General Household Survey, and their support should also be acknowledged.

INTRODUCTION

KEY QUESTIONS

This book is about the contribution of the social sciences, particularly anthropology and sociology, to an understanding of old age. It seeks to advance our understanding of the world we live in by studying the position of old age within it. The key questions this book poses are: What are the universal characteristics, if any, of the ageing experience? In what different ways is it possible to grow old? What is unique and special about old age in the contemporary world? Answering these questions will illuminate the way we understand society as a whole. It could be argued that the most significant change in modern society lies in its age structure. The period starting from about the last third of the twentieth century has seen the development of new kinds of societies in which one-fifth to a quarter of the population are retired, where fewer babies are born than are required to sustain the size of the population and which see most people living until they are over 80 years of age. There is a strong case that the essential, archetypical characteristic of the modern condition is that of old age.

This book explores the social construction of old age and seeks to develop an understanding of 'old age' as a cultural category. As a consequence there is no simple definition of 'old age' as a starting point. Rather the book explores the way old age becomes a meaningful cultural category to different social groups in different historical and social situations. To do this we need to look not only at the variety of content to the category 'old age', but also at the boundaries between what comes before and what follows old age and the processes of transition of entering and leaving the social identity. We can ask: How do we know about growing older? The collectivity – the 'we' in this question – could be construed as we, the readers as individuals. How do we gain knowledge about ourselves and our ageing? The term might also be taken to denote a social and cultural collective 'we' – the dominant social, cultural and scientific understanding of old age used by people in the 'West'.[1] In order to do this we must look at the ways in which social, economic and political institutions – together with cultural values, images and knowledge about ageing bodies – are created and sustained by people. People exist in particular times and places and are therefore subject to the social influences of their past, of their contemporaries and of their futures. How is the experience of old age embedded in the past? How is old age being transformed in the present? And what influence does knowledge about the future have on our present view of old age? The book will discuss how old age becomes a meaningful concept which people, both the general public and gerontological experts of all kinds, use to explain and understand themselves and those around them. If 'old age' and our understanding of it are a product of society, the logical questions are: How are they different in different societies? How do different cultural traditions, in particular those current in the modern societies of the North/industrial/capitalist/urban world, construct our understanding of old age? The prime focus of this book is to look at the advanced industrial nations of the West. However, in order to understand the societies and cultures in which the majority of readers of this book are located, we must also reflect on different and contrasting situations.

Individual ageing is universal but does not necessarily lead to an ageing population. Ageing populations are a relatively new phenomenon in anthropological terms. There are entirely different social processes by which individuals and societies are said to age. On the one hand there is the experience that everyone who gets older has. Those who reach 'old age' have this experience in common – an individual experience of getting old and being old. That is the subject of the first chapter of this book. On the other hand the ageing of societies is about population change and reflects alterations in the relative size of age groups in the population. One definition of an ageing population is one with an increasing average age. However, it is important to differentiate the experience of individuals ageing on the one hand, and the causes and social impact of ageing populations on the other. People have always aged, but an ageing population in which the average age of the population is rising steadily into middle age is a new phenomenon. Growing old as an individual in a young population and growing old in a population that already has a high proportion of older people clearly result in different opportunities and problems.

There is a strong temptation to reification, whereby the social characteristics of individuals are assumed to be the social characteristics of societies. It is assumed that a society which is 'old' in the sense of having a high average age also has the characteristics of an older human being – their personality, attitudes, aspirations and capabilities. This is of course a mistake; societies are not individuals and they do not have personalities or personal attributes, they have institutional practices and common ways of behaving. Further inaccuracies develop because not only are individual characteristics reified to a societal level but those characteristics identified are stereotypical and ageist. Hence societies with older populations are sometimes denigrated as being tied by tradition, unproductive, lacking in innovation and even tending to 'senility'.

Throughout this book we will deal with both aspects of old age, the personal and the societal. In each of the six chapters the book will examine the origins and consequences of distinctive features of old age in the contemporary world and demonstrate both the diversity and inequality that are the experience of older people. The chapters are as follows:

Chapter 1, entitled 'The experience of old age', sets out to demonstrate the manner in which we come to view ourselves as old. It looks at the interpersonal processes by which we recognise old age in ourselves and in others. It examines the ways in which particular cultural constructions of old age have become prevalent in Western society. Further, it provides comparative material to illustrate that the same constructions of old age are not to be found universally, but rather that there is a wide diversity of experience of old age across the world. Among these patterns of diversity are the inequalities and disparity in standards of living that older people experience.

Chapter 2 is based on discussion of historical and contemporary changes to the life course. This includes consideration of family, friendship, kinship, community and work patterns and how they have changed between and through different life courses. Issues of gender, class, ethnicity and migration are incorporated into this discussion. The life-course approach which links historical processes, personal biography and social structure is a key tool in understanding not only old age but contemporary society as a whole. The importance for social science in understanding life-course processes, in particular the experiences of successive generations and their interactions, is drawn out.

Chapter 3 examines the impact on older people of the global crises of poverty, environment and population. It looks at the extent and causes of old-age poverty in the world, and the range of insecurities which older people can experience. Population ageing is not only the experience of the developed world but a global phenomenon.

Chapter 4 concentrates on inequality in old age and inter-generational conflict. Provision for a secure old age can be made either through the state and citizenship or through private property and pension funds. This chapter looks at the issues of pension fund capitalism, the role of the state in the provision of a 'good old age' and the fundamental issues of social solidarity which underpin the willingness to sustain social groups who do not have paid employment.

Consumerism, identity and old age are the subject of Chapter 5. This chapter tackles the issues that are raised by relative affluence for some older people and by the commercialisation of old age. It covers the topics of:

- The distinctive characteristics of older consumers.
- The meaning of consumption for older people.
- The institutions of consumption; how does the way consumption is organised affect older people?
- The problems and opportunities that the changing technology of consumption creates for older people.

Medical and biological conceptualisations of ageing have come to dominate the modern understanding of old age. Chapter 6 looks at old age, sickness, death and immortality. The concept of the 'third age' as a new time of life involving the prolongation of youth and a new post-work identity will be deconstructed and the problems of the 'fourth age' as the final part of the life course before death examined. The relationship between the medicalisation of old age and views of immortality are also examined and insights derived from the sociology of the body are applied to the ageing body. This chapter explores the significance for old age of 'death' debates – euthanasia and genetically postponed mortality. The Conclusion draws together the key points of the book and in particular contrasts optimistic and pessimistic visions for the future of old age.

1

THE EXPERIENCE OF OLD AGE

The Patriarch: *We came slowly up the track from Konjic, past the meadows sweeping back to the dark conifers which covered the mountains. Along past the old rustic poles fencing the paddocks and into a small group of wooden farm houses. We picked our way through the narrow cobbled alleys to ask for Mohammed Ibrahamivic. We were shown into the large kitchen-cum-living room and sat on the sofa. Strong coffee and black-currant juice was served and we explained our purpose – to ask him to tell us his life story. The large, busy, woman in the kitchen organised everything. He arrived and settled down opposite us and the tape recorder. In came three men of various ages, more women and many children. Mohammed was quiet but fit and strong, over 78 but firmly in charge. He told us how he was born and raised in a big family some kilometres away; how he survived the war by keeping his head down; about his marriage – joking at his small wife tucked in the corner of the crowded room. He detailed his family – including the twenty-four people in the room and the rest around about the village or in Germany. He listed with some help all his many grandchildren. He joked about old age, and made it clear he was still fit and still felt frisky when he saw a young maid. Here was a man who was able to present his old age to us as fulfilment.*

THE SOCIAL CONSTRUCTION OF OLD AGE

When, where and how do people begin to think of themselves as old? The same questions may be asked about how others are identified as 'old'. This chapter is about the social construction of old age. If something is described as 'ageing', what is being denoted is an organisation of time; a sequence of stages. It refers to the timing and sequencing in some specified process. With human beings, it is ageing which gives the individual's life its rhythm, and links the duration, timing and sequence of stages in life. It is the social sequencing of the stages that creates the category 'old age' and gives the life course its meaning.

There are approaches to old age that concentrate on the individual experience of ageing. These perspectives seek an understanding of old age using as reference points one's own former (younger) self and in particular other people's reaction to the individual ageing persona we express. The 'mask of ageing' describes the experience whereby there is felt to be a distance between one's interior age and the externally manifest ageing appearance which is seen in the mirror and to which other people respond.[1] This chapter will start by looking at the social practices by which old age is constructed at the level of interpersonal interaction and then move on to the cultural significance attributed to old age. We can ask a very basic question: How do people know how old they are?

SOCIAL REGULATION OF AGE IN BRITAIN

People know their age from the way other people behave towards them. Most significantly people in Britain know because their family celebrate their birthday and have done so since they were born. Every year they mark the passing of another year with cards and presents, perhaps a party or other forms of celebration. Its importance is symbolically marked by ritual. Key birthdays, for example, the twenty-first or one-hundredth, are particularly ritualised. To have one's birthday forgotten is deeply hurtful and to have no one who knows or cares when it is marks a nadir in social isolation. Thus it seems very odd for those raised in the British cultural tradition that some people do not know how old they are. It is hard to understand that in many cultures and societies it is not of significance and people simply have no reason to remember their exact chronological age. Birth dates, even if they are known, are not universally counted or celebrated. In the Slav tradition it is on one's 'Slava' – the day of one's saint – when one is expected to give presents to others. Social time is constructed ritually. These rituals create special moments which break up and pattern the uniform flow of time. They may be counted and used to mark transition from one life stage to another and indeed can be used to create a sense of historical identity and continuity.[2]

People in the West know their age because society regulates public life according to chronological age. Age is not only ritualised but it is also bureaucratised. There are legal rights and duties based on age. Institutions regulate access and prescribe and proscribe certain behaviours by age. As a consequence it becomes important for the state to officially register births and thus certificate age. Other institutions also certificate age; for example, bus companies issue passes to schoolchildren and to older people to regulate access to cheap fares. Public houses and licensing authorities introduce card schemes to regulate age-based restrictions on the purchase of alcohol. The institutional arrangements of modern society require us to be able to demonstrate our age to others.

The boundary between the roles of child and adult is linked to the acquisition of age-defined rights and duties. The age at which people have been considered to be adult and what is meant by being a child has changed through time. There are specific ages at which people are considered to be personally responsible for their actions. The law sets ages of criminal responsibility, to legally have sex or to drive a car. Other aspects of social responsibility – the legal right to leave home, obtain housing benefit, get married or leave school – are restricted by age. Civic responsibility, in the form of military service, the right to vote and duty to serve on a jury, is also regulated by age criteria. At the opposite end of the life course age criteria can come back into play. Over a certain age (70), you are required to renew your driving licence every 3 years and if you have a disability you must have a doctor certify that you are fit to drive. Further, you are entitled to certain benefits by virtue of age – a free television licence after the age of 75 and the right to priority housing under the Homeless Persons Act. Age-based legal restrictions exclude people from work-related benefits such as incapacity benefit. In Britain, you are excused from jury service if over the age of 70. Such institutional arrangements play a part in allocating people into the category 'old'.

THE IMPORTANCE OF PENSIONS IN ESTABLISHING THE MODERN CATEGORY 'OLD AGE'

The single most important transition that is seen to mark entry into old age is retirement. In contemporary Britain the terms 'pensioner' and 'older person' are used almost interchangeably. Even my 12-year-old dog was described as a 'pensioner' when a fellow dog walker contrasted her to the puppy she was exercising. However, retirement is a modern phenomenon and in the twentieth century it has come to dominate our thinking about and understanding of old age.[3] It is modern both in the sense of a historically recent phenomenon, and in the sense that it is characteristic of the kind of society that has been labelled 'modern' – specifically the urban, industrial societies of Western Europe and North America. In pre-modern times people were perceived as old at the age at which they ceased to be independent, economically or physically, and this varied among individuals. The modern structure of the working life has segmented the life course into pre-work, work and post-work phases.[4] The conventional definition of chronological old age as starting at 60 or 65 stems from standardisation and bureaucratisation of the life course around the administration of retirement pensions. This contrasts with the situation in more traditional rural environments. For example, the transition between generations in the rural west of Ireland in the 1930s, described by Arensberg was clearly marked and ritualised by the 'match'.[5] This was a formal agreement whereby the inheriting son would marry at the same time as the elderly couple would hand on the property. Traditionally the 'old couple' would reserve themselves a room and produce from the smallholding to see them through their retirement.

Historical research suggests that, in Britain, the definition of old age in pre-modern times was individual and flexible but that over a period from about 1850 to 1950 a new, more rigid definition of old age developed. Over this time fixed retirement ages have become the norm and the association between a person's physical condition and their giving up work, or at least paid employment, has lessened. Thane argues that before the early nineteenth century individuals retired from their occupations at whatever age they felt unable to carry them out.[6] The rationale of those developing fixed retirement ages illustrates the forces at play in establishing the modern concept of old age. In Britain the first fixed retirement age was introduced in 1859 for civil servants and was set at the age of 65. The establishment of a widely uniform age of transition from work to retirement created the norm of the older person as someone without occupation and the conventional association of the age 65 with old age.

A peculiarity of the British pension system is the differential age of retirement for men and women. Women retire at age 60, five years before men, despite their greater longevity.[7] The Second World War pension reforms saw the lowering of women's pensionable age to 60. This decision followed an effective national campaign by the National Spinsters Association and was argued on the basis that women received poorer wages than did men. Further, the system assumed a married couple and paid the wife's pension on the basis of the husband's National Insurance contributions at his retirement, not on the basis of her age. As women tended to marry older men, spinsters would typically draw their pensions later than married women and this was seen as unfair.[8] In more recent years, the practice of standardised retirement ages has become less rigid. Two factors have been influential in these changes which developed through the last quarter of the twentieth century. First, there is the use of early retirement to manage fluctuations in the labour market, and using pensions to attract older workers to withdraw from paid employment. Second, there is the cultural re-evaluation of the post-work phase of life known as the 'third age' in which the positive attractions and opportunities for personal growth in retirement have been highlighted.

The regulation of state benefits by age is also reflected in commercial discounts for children and pensioners. The assumption that old age means reduced income prompts restaurants, cinemas and bingo halls to offer special rates for those who can show their pension book. However, these formal and institutional methods of regulation are only a small part of how chronological age enters consciousness and influences behaviour. The whole of the life course is structured around cultural expectations of appropriate behaviour for people of particular ages. Two factors are at work here. The first is the structure of mass society in which large-scale organisations regulate people's lives. Education is structured by age; at school, university and other institutions one is processed in units recruited by age. The second factor is the 'generation gap' feature, by which rapid social change creates different experiences and values in different cohorts. This has the consequence that people of different 'generations' have specific cultural attributes ranging from fashions in music and clothes to attitudes towards sex and marriage. Hence the twentieth century has seen increasing social segregation around age groups. Housing has become more age segregated, consumption and taste more differentiated. This age-related behaviour can be seen when, either deliberately (as with breaching experiments in the manner of Garfinkel[9]), or inadvertently (through accident or ignorance), people confound the social expectations of age and appear at the

wrong place or the wrong time and behave in culturally inappro-
priate ways.

SOCIAL CUES TO OLD AGE

Research by David Karp in America has demonstrated some of
the bases through which people tend to become conscious of
growing old.[10] His research is based on qualitative interviews
with male and female professionals, and reveals the manner in
which his informants learned about their age through the ways
other people treated them. Karp's informants report that these
signals of old age are not always welcome and not necessarily
internalised; interviewees often felt like strangers to themselves.
This experience is commonly discussed under the label the 'mask
of ageing' and refers to the feeling of there being a youthful inner
self masked by an external ageing body. Thus Karp's first category
of cues to ageing is 'body reminders'. These are the kinds of
illnesses – prostrate problems, arthritis, and aspects of body
performance such as snoring, or perhaps loss of fitness – which
alert people to an awareness of 'getting old'. These bodily signs,
including fitness and health, are identified as first raising a
consciousness of ageing.

There are symbolic calendrical cues to 'old age'. Some
informants identified the significance of age 50 as a mid-point
of a hundred years. The idea is that the half-century marks the
top of a cycle – 'it is downhill after 50'. Respondents felt they
had to count the time they had left; they ceased to pay prime
attention to the time since they set out on life's journey. Karp
identifies what he calls 'generational reminders' which cue his
respondents into old age. Their relationship to their parents,
specifically if their parents are growing frail or starting to die,
is an important generational reminder of approaching old age for
themselves. Being left behind as the oldest member of the family
brings an inescapable sense of old age. Approaching the ages
at which their parents die can also alert people to a consciousness of approaching the final stage of life. Intergenerational

relationships with children mirror those with parents. The sense of growing old comes as part and parcel of the experience of children marrying and having children of their own. The achievement of grandparenthood is seen by many to be particularly significant. It is a distinctive role that is associated with old age (although of course in terms of chronological age most people become grandparents in their middle years – their fifties). These changing relationships also bring with them a realisation of a distance, both socially and culturally, from their children and people of their children's age.

Individuals begin to appreciate their own ageing by becoming aware of their relationship to people around them. This occurs not only at home in a domestic and kinship environment but also at work and in social life more generally. Karp calls these 'contextual reminders'. Becoming the oldest at work, or in a context such as a club or voluntary organisation, is noted by people and their significant others. The senior workman is turned to for knowledge of the tradition of the firm; the longest-serving member is custodian of the history of the organisation or workplace. In the House of Commons the role of the longest-serving member is institutionalised in the role of the Father of the House. Reaching that position, one can no longer harbour illusions of one's self as the rising star of the organisation, or the 'young Turk' setting out to change the firm. One of Karp's informants was an older doctor who described how his sense of being old developed as his patient group grew older with him. Teachers saw students becoming further and further distanced from themselves in terms of age. Important in this distancing effect were modes of dress and references to acting and speaking one's age. People are cued by others as to age-appropriate behaviour and this is generally internalised, although as in all social life there are deviant resisters. People are not simple social dupes but when they do choose to ignore social convention they are made aware that this is what they are doing.

The key defining characteristic of old age is that it is the stage of life next to death. The whole relationship between death and old age will be explored in greater depth in Chapter 6. Reminders of people's mortality cue them into an awareness of their ageing. Life-threatening illnesses such as cancer and heart disease in friends and relatives heightened Karp's informants' own sense of mortality. These illnesses are sharp indicators to people themselves that they have entered a time of life with higher expectations of mortality. An understanding that there is limited time left to live out one's life is the last of Karp's categories of cues to ageing. The finiteness of one's lifetime becomes pressing; life projects, work projects need to be accomplished in the limited time that is left. People aware of ageing asked themselves questions such as 'What can I achieve in my last five years of work?' The realisation that one has only limited time left can be a turning point in people's careers and lifestyles. The realisation brings to an end preparation for life to come, and may stimulate new behaviour and new activities stemming from the idea of beginning a new phase in life. This is sometimes expressed as a mid-life crisis, sometimes as the liberation of the fifties. It may be expressed as the way in which accumulated wisdom and life experience leads to a fuller existence. Perhaps this is seen in terms of relationships, enjoying the 'empty nest', relief from the responsibilities of adult family life and full-time parenting. It is noted that some men become more feminine, women more masculine; men want to reconnect with family, women to revive careers – people look to achieve new roles, to make a different mark on the stage in the final act before the curtain comes down.

A CROSS-CULTURAL COMPARISON OF THE CONSTRUCTION OF OLD AGE

Karp's account of the cues to approaching old age resonate with those of us who are old enough to experience them. They are however culturally, and in many ways class and gender, specific. In so far as contrasting social groups experience work and family life differently, so the salience of different cues to one's 'age' identity will also differ. It is possible to examine other ways in which old age is experienced by drawing on fieldwork I conducted in Bosnia in 1991 before the destruction of that society by violent nationalisms.[11] One of the purposes of the research was to understand how differently old age was constructed and experienced in a cultural context which contrasted with the UK. One theme which kept repeating itself in discussions of old age with informants was a loss of 'power'. This idea of old age as loss of 'vital force' is more appropriate for a society without regular retirement and institutionalised age-based roles. In these circumstances individual feelings are more likely to be salient to defining old age than other criteria such as mere years or even external appearance. The nearest equivalent in Britain is perhaps the perception of one of Thompson, Itzin and Abendstern's respondents who is quoted as describing herself as 'slowing down'.[12] This phrase is instantly recognisable as a meaningful conceptualisation of old age in Britain.

In Bosnia it was widely stated that ageing could be detected by loss of *snaga*. *Snaga* is a difficult word to translate.[13] It means 'power', 'force', but it has a positive connotation such that perhaps 'vigour' might be an appropriate translation into English. Yet in Serbo-Croatian, political parties or military hit squads can be described using the same term. Asked to specify those cues which identified to themselves their status as 'old', the most common reply was 'I have loss my *snaga*' ('I have lost my strength'). This response would be elaborated with comments such as 'I can't do things like I did them before' or sometimes 'I feel weak, slow'. For example, one very elderly lady from Maglaj explained that she did not have any *snaga* 'power' any more. She said she was most happy when the weather was good and she could work outside. In other words she did not have the 'force' to work outside in bad weather as she used to. This idea is not limited to rural or non-professional circles. A medical doctor attending a seminar given on the social definitions of old age advanced his hypothesis of ageing – that it involved loss of *snaga* power – and he believed that this was due to the wearing out of the digestive system which prevented old people from getting the energy they needed.

It is clear that *snaga* refers to both social and physical strength, and that both of these are entailed in the experience of my Bosnian informants. Loss of 'power' has psychological and social status implications and these are experienced as the same, and expressed with the idea of loss of *snaga*. The onset of physical dependency can be associated with a psychological sense of loss of energy as the elderly person takes less responsibility for family decisions. This leads to a diminished ability to take the initiative in determining collective behaviour. The accompanying loss of fully adult status, namely becoming a dependant, means loss of social power. This analysis may be linked to the frequent association of inability to work and of ill-health with the idea of old age in Bosnia, whereas the association of old age with a yearly chronology is seldom made. There is no simple mechanism of attribution by which physical disability leads to lowering of social status. The obedience, respect and care due from children and daughters-in-law is widely acknowledged as a normative expectation. In reality the development of economic and physical dependency leads to changes in social relationships, internal to the family, which are experienced by the elderly person as 'loss'. This 'loss' is of course a relative concept; people may still be relatively fit but experience loss of *snaga* when compared to their previous position, when they were 'in their prime' and at the peak of the family cycle. In the rural extended family situation, while they are fit and able to work, at whatever age, the senior generation still keeps control and has highest status in the household. Physical impairment which leads to dependency, whatever the age, leads to loss of status and 'power'.

STANDARD OF LIVING AND QUALITY OF LIFE IN OLD AGE

A common experience of growing old is loss of income. The changing material circumstances of older people are a further example of the impact of social institutions on old age. The possibilities of living a satisfactory old age are severely constrained by how much money they have. Many older people, even in the developed world, continue to live in relative poverty.

For Europe (as defined by twelve members of the European Union), Walker and Maltby summarise the main trends in material standards as:

- rising living standards for older people, particularly those aged 50 to 74;
- wide variations between countries;
- poverty and low incomes among a significant minority of older people in most countries;
- older women, particularly widows, having a higher incidence of poverty;
- growing income inequalities among pensioners.[14]

There is evidence to show that in Britain there is a growing number of old people who are significantly more affluent than was typical a generation ago.[15] However, the fact also remains that, on average, older people have significantly less spending power than most other age groups in society. In 1979 the average income of the poorest 20 per cent of pensioners in the UK was £55.90 per week, compared with £169.60 for the richest 20 per cent. Sixteen years later, the average income of the poorest 20 per cent had risen by £15.50 but the average income of the richest 20 per cent had risen by £103.40.[16] At the start of the twenty-first century, a quarter of all older people in Britain are either dependent on income support or entitled to that benefit but not receiving it.

In the UK, using the General Household Survey for 1998, it is possible to show that although it is clear that some pensioners have become significantly better off than in the past, there is still a large pool of pensioner poverty.[17] The General Household Survey records weekly household income and also the number of adults in households. Per capita weekly household income seems a reasonable index to compare older people's incomes as it takes into account the pooling of income between earners and non-earners, although clearly this involves large, and in some cases possibly unwarranted, assumptions. The General Household Survey is sufficiently large to make comparisons of age groups meaningful. When looking at income distributions, very high incomes of a few individuals tend to skew average figures upward. The median is a useful figure because it is the mid-point, and indicates the income level below which the poorest 50 per cent fall and the richest 50 per cent exceed (Table 1.1).

The median pensioner income is half that of non-pensioners. The survey reports the total percentage of households without pensioners as being 67 per cent. Households with no pensioners make up 52 per cent of the poorest 10 per cent while they make up 93.3 per cent of the richest 10 per cent. Over three-quarters of those in the top 10 per cent of incomes are aged between 30 and 59 while around one-third of the bottom 10 per cent fall into the same age category.[18] One definition of poverty is to be living in a household with less than 60 per cent of the average (median) income (Table 1.2).

In the USA income inequalities tend to be greater. However, despite the different income maintenance and welfare regimes, a pattern whereby older, female and minority groups have the

Table 1.1 Median per capita weekly household income (£s)

	All	Non-pensioner households	One-pensioner households	Two-pensioner households
Mean	237.37	277.40	143.06	133.73
Median	183.37	229.82	112.80	105.54
Bottom 10%	71.35	77.75	69.48	64.05
Bottom 20%	91.93	117.80	75.00	74.21
Top 10%	438.46	484.54	251.33	226.87

Source: Office for National Statistics Social Survey Division, *General Household Survey*, 1998–1999 (computer file), 2nd edn. Colchester: UK Data Archive, 3 April 2001, SN: 4134.

Table 1.2 Percentage of group with less than 60 per cent of the median household income; age, gender and ethnicity

		All	Men	Women	Non-white
Under 65	No. in sample	2835	1222	1613	369
	% within age group	18.9	16.6	21.1	32.2
65–69	No. in sample	396	167	229	8[a]
	% within age group	46.8	40.6	52.6	42.1
70–74	No. in sample	434	178	256	4[a]
	% within age group	56.7	49.9	62.6	40.0
75–79	No. in sample	412	157	255	2[a]
	% within age group	65.6	59.7	69.9	28.6
80–84	No. in sample	218	75	143	1[a]
	% within age group	71.0	62.5	76.5	100.0
85 and over	No. in sample	144	48	96	1[a]
	% within age group	70.6	68.6	71.6	100.0
All ages	No. in sample	4439	1847	2592	385
	% within age group	25.0	21.5	28.2	32.5

Source: Office for National Statistics Social Survey Division, *General Household Survey, 1998–1999* (computer file), 2nd edn, Colchester: UK Data Archive, 3 April 2001, SN: 4134, n = 17,780.
Note: [a] These numbers are too small to be interpreted meaningfully but do reflect the small size of the minority elder population in the UK.

lowest incomes is also found. Using data from the US Social Security Administration Table 1.3 illustrates the proportions of men and women from different ethnic groups who fall below the official US poverty line.

Some American commentators have suggested that the poverty line is not a good measure because it is pitched at the level which excludes a large number of older people who have minimal resources that take them just above the level where they would be eligible for benefits.[19] If we include all people whose incomes are not more than 20 per cent above the poverty line, the proportion of those older people who might be considered poor goes up

Table 1.3 Percentage of age group by gender and race which falls below the official US poverty line

By race	White: percentage below poverty line	Black: percentage below poverty line	Hispanic origin: percentage below poverty line
All persons			
65–69	7.2	16.8	18.9
70–74	8.1	22.6	19.0
75–79	9.8	22.4	17.6
80–84	10.3	27.8	22.2
85 or older	12.1	33.8	15.9
Men			
65–69	5.9	13.5	21.3
70–74	6.8	13.0	18.6
75–79	6.2	16.8	12.0
80–84	6.7	22.6	20.0
85 or older	8.0	37.1	[a]
Women			
65–69	8.3	19.5	17.1
70–74	9.2	27.6	19.3
75–79	12.3	25.9	21.1
80–84	12.8	32.1	23.6
85 or older	14.2	32.1	21.4

Source: Social Security Administration (2002) Income of the Population 55 or Older, 2000, accessible at <http://www.ssa.gov/statistics/incpop55/2000/sect8.pdf>
Note: [a] Sample proportion too small for reliable calculation.

for all groups aged 65 and over from 10.2 per cent to 16.9 per cent. The equivalent figures for 'whites 85 and over' increase from 12.1 per cent to 24.1 per cent and for 'blacks 85 and over' from 33.8 per cent to 48.2 per cent.

It is important to distinguish between observed indices of inequalities in income and wealth and the perceptions older people have of their financial condition. Older people have a number of possible reference groups against whom they can compare their own condition. If they look at the experience of their parents, or older people they knew as they grew into adulthood, for most older people their current condition compares favourably. If however they compare themselves to the rest of the population regardless of their age, these comparisons are much less favourable. Similarly, in the UK less convivial comparisons may be made with other pensioners in other European states. Finally pensioners are far from equal in their material circumstances and a pensioner's view of their own affluence, or lack of it, may be made by comparison to other pensioners.

There is considerable evidence to show that inequalities experienced during the life course are reflected in greater measure in an unequal old age. The material circumstances of older people are profoundly affected by their ability to earn during their working lives. To this end the relatively poor pay and lack of work opportunities afforded to women, to minorities, to the disabled and to others results in a lack of pensions and income in old age. The recent gains in pensioner income have been largely around the maturing of work-based earnings-related pension schemes. They clearly benefit those with a continuous and well-paid work history, and in particular male professionals. In Britain the arguments about cultural diversity are built on increased prosperity in old age.

> Orthodox social gerontology has treated later life as if it were constituted by inventories of social need and social exclusion. This is not how older people live and experience their lives. The growth of retirement as a third age – a potential crown of life – has been constructed primarily in terms of leisure and self-fulfilment. While these practices may be most fully enacted by a relatively small section of the population of older people, culturally this group represents the aspirations of many whether or not they are able to realize such lifestyle.[20]

However, this group is also generationally specific. Their prosperity is built around occupational pensions and owner-occupied housing. The 1998/9 General Household Survey indicates that nearly 50 per cent (49.1 per cent) of 61- to 70-year-olds are owner occupiers and that they or their spouses are in receipt of an occupational pension. The equivalent figure for those aged over 80 is only 28 per cent. This is not a simple age phenomenon. It is a complex generational phenomenon built on the economic and political circumstances through which these generations lived. Not only has there been a general rise in the value of earnings and employment, there have been changes in legislation, which have significantly advantaged home ownership. Housing policies in Britain since the 1960s have removed protected tenure for those renting, given the right to buy to council tenants, given significant tax advantages and financial incentives to owner occupiers, and made home ownership the best investment opportunity for most people in Britain. Different generations have been financially advantaged or disadvantaged by these changes. Family and household patterns have also changed over the generations, in particular with more single-person households. These changes have also had impacts on changing values of property and access to housing over the lifetime of specific cohorts, advantaging those who are now the 'young old' and disadvantaging those who are currently the 'old old'. Similarly the employment experience of specific generations, particularly the generation which first started work in the 1950s and 1960s, has been significantly better than their predecessors, and they have benefited from changes in pension legislation, and in particular the introduction of earnings-related pensions. It is clear that there is a cohort impact on the diversity of economic well-being in old age in Britain. Further, that these differences cannot be understood merely as a result of individual choice or a prudent life course but have to be seen within a framework of the political and economic circumstances through which the cohorts lived.

WOMEN AND WIDOWS

The differential life courses experienced by men and women result in differences in their experience of ageing. Women in old age experience particular problems in maintaining a reasonable standard of living. There are combinations of biological and social differences between the genders that lead to women living longer than men in most societies. It is common to find a higher proportion of widows compared to widowers. This is not only because more men die before their wives but because widowed men commonly remarry and women do so much less often. It has been argued by de Beauvoir and others that there is a 'double jeopardy' of age and gender.[21] For women who are also older, the risks of marginalisation and deprivation are significantly greater. For example, economic development can have differential consequences for older women compared to older men. Barbara Rogers, among others, has demonstrated a gender bias in development programmes which has implications for older women.[22]

Access to work and its benefits is one major factor in the gender inequalities in old age. In most countries there is an emphasis on paid employment as the basis for pensions and welfare systems; for example contributions systems are organised through employers. Given the characteristics of the workforce in the modern sectors of the global economy, women, old people and those living in rural areas are the ones most systematically excluded. Older women in rural areas tend to be among the most materially deprived people in most countries. Many older people in the developing world where there is little provision for pensions find it necessary to look for work to support themselves in old age. The limited evidence available suggests that fewer older women are a part of the labour force than older men. For example, in Peru some 75 per cent of men aged 60 to 64 participate in the labour force, compared to just 24 per cent of women of the same age.[23] This does not mean that older women actually work less than men do, but simply that the work they do is less likely to be in the formal sector. Older women may be involved in agricultural work, childcare and household duties, or small-scale trading. While important and often demanding, many of these types of work are not recognised by communities or in official statistics, and do not receive the cash rewards of work defined as male.

In so far as women are confined to the domestic sphere and become dependent on their husbands and families, this can create potential problems in widowhood. In the West the establishment of widows' pensions was an early form of insurance created frequently through self-help institutions. In many societies institutions such as widow inheritance ensure substitute families for widows, although it is far from clear that this is always in the best interests of the widows.[24] In India, the position of widows has raised a number of concerns. Two institutions have an impact on this issue. First, the patrilineal extended family based around a group of close male relatives makes incoming wives to some extent strangers in the family. Second, the conceptualisation of the husband-and-wife relationship as permanent (even eternal) and having a particularly sacred quality creates in its counterpart, widowhood, a particularly defiling condition. According to Dr Indira Jai Prakash, widowhood in India is regarded as 'social death', with constraints on dress, diet and public behaviour that isolate women.[25] Her research indicated that households headed by widows suffer dramatic decline in per capita income and that the mortality risk of widowhood was higher for women than for men. It is suggested that among basic causes of widows' vulnerability in India are the restrictions on residence inheritance, remarriage and employment opportunities.[26]

EXPECTATIONS OF OLD AGE

The life course consists of a pattern of normative transitions across the idealised life span. In other words it is a set of expectations about how the life course should develop. Young children may say to their parents 'I am not going to get married', or 'I am not going to have children', but the vast majority eventually do so. What is more, those who do not choose marriage and children nevertheless carry the social consequences of having departed from those typical expectations. These patterns of expectation may be identified in, among others, family, work, residential and religious spheres. Chapter 5 contains an extended discussion around the idea that contemporary social change is altering these expectations and making them less rigid.

Somewhat independent of these normative expectations are the actual behaviours by which people go through life, the age at which, in practice, they marry, have children, start work, retire, are baptised or confirmed, buy a house or retire to the seaside. Not only do social expectations change but people's preferences and values alter their willingness to live non-conforming ways of life. The constraints that structure the possibility of making life-course choices influence the chances of fulfilling a normative life course. If a war wipes out the men of a generation, women's family life-course patterns will have to change. If a large baby-boom generation monopolises the available work opportunities, it may be more difficult for the successor cohorts to find suitable work and follow the expected work trajectories through life. The interplay between normative expectations and social change can be illustrated with the example of the consequence of the changing patterns of life expectancy through the twentieth century. This demographic change has meant that the meaning and experience of married life has changed. For example, the significance of child-rearing for married life has altered:

> the time that couples spend alone after the last child has left home has been extended from 1.6 years in the early 1900s to 12.9 years in the 1970s, an increase of over 11 years. This means that where previously the death of a spouse usually occurred less than 2 years after the 1st child married, now married couples can plan on staying together for 13 years after their last child has left home.[27]

Thus a new period has come to be named and discussed by demographers and social scientists – the so-called 'empty nest' stage in the family life course. The values of married life need not have changed for the changed demographic parameters to alter the meaning of 'till death do us part'. People come to old age with a family, work, housing history, together with a lifetime of unfolding faith and leisure activities. The implications for understanding old age as the product not merely of a normative life course but the social changes and the opportunities available and closed off during the personal history are profound. Such a view bypasses simplistic notions for explaining social behaviour. The condition of old age is neither the result of free will and individual agency nor of social or genetic determinism. Family, work, domestic and residential life, religious and cultural experience unfold as people age and chart a course through the perils of life and the currents of social change. Members of society are part of the crew struggling to keep the ship afloat in the tides of history and those in old age have been on the voyage longest.

The term 'natural' has a range of meanings. It can be used in the sense of 'obvious' or to mean 'taken for granted'. If age is a 'natural' phenomenon then there is a tendency for certain behaviours to be seen as 'normal' for people of certain ages. 'Natural' has a further meaning that comes from the concept of 'the natural world'. Thus there is a temptation to think of age-based categories as if they were biological rather than social divisions. This is potentially dangerous as it gives these categories an immutable normality. The study of old age should not assume there is a 'normal old age' but rather examine the impact of assumptions that such a normality exists. The list of social divisions which are commonly labelled 'natural' include sex, race and age. Social scientists have developed a vocabulary that emphasises the social as opposed to biological distinctions. Thus gender is referred to rather than sex; ethnicity preferred to race. Social science has yet to develop a similar terminological differentiation to distinguish the various possible referents for age. There is no readily available vocabulary through which linguistic distinctions are drawn between calendrical age, biological age, social or psychological age.

It is a commonplace that we are dying from the moment we are born. Ageing is a process of coming closer to death, and it starts at the beginning. However, there are differences in the ways bodily change is understood and valued with increasing age. Some changes such as the acquisition of language, growing taller and the manifestations of sexual maturity through puberty are thought of as development and positively evaluated. Maturity is judged against a putative 'prime of life'. Other changes such the menopause or changes in bone composition in later life are seen as loss and decline. Loss of *snaga* for Bosnians is one aspect of a wider feeling across cultures that old age is associated with loss. Spencer identifies a universal problem of loss through ageing and says that the universality is not simply biological but cultural, environmental and psychological.[28] Spencer argues that the so-called 'prime of life' can be seen as the stable and most integrated part of the life course psychologically;[29] the achievement of social recognition and adult status; and the peak of physical condition. He suggests that this is most often characterised as lasting from about 18 to 30 years of age. However, others would be more circumspect about the timing, merely pointing out a pre-'old age' peak to the trajectory of life. Further, whether the social, psychological and biological 'prime' coincide chronologically is open to challenge. Certainly there is an extremely wide range in cultural variation in these aspects of ageing. Biological change takes place throughout the life course; in the early years this is usually referred to as maturation, in later years as ageing. Biologically, ageing is associated with a number of bodily changes but the process is a long one, and various human features wane at different rates and in different ways. Spencer sees a 'natural life span'; thus there is a subsequent period in the life course when the organism, human or otherwise, is less than it was in its prime. Therefore, from his perspective, all humans experience a time when feelings of weakness and of 'slowing down' occur in contrast to one's former condition. Hence, it is not a *particular* set of physical or social conditions but rather the feeling of loss, which Spencer argues is the universal experience of ageing. The problem of 'loss' appears as a fairly universal attribute of ageing; as discussed above, the culturally specific manifestations of those feelings in Bosnia are expressed through the phrase 'loss of *snaga*'.

It is possible to argue that an individual's feelings about their age have to reconcile the status of adulthood and the experience of physical changes associated with advancing years. It may be argued further that this interaction is required across cultures even though the culturally based concepts of old age, adulthood and of physical condition and bodily appearance may be varied. Thompson, Itzin and Abendstern discuss these issues in a British context.[30] It is clear from their work that elderly people in Britain have to manage a discrepancy between the cultural expectations of the elderly and their own feelings about themselves.

> You can feel old at any point in adulthood. Men and women in their twenties or thirties or forties can feel they have failed to find the right person to marry, or have made the wrong career choice, and that they are 'too old' to start again. Feeling old is feeling exhausted in spirit, lacking the energy to find new responses as life changes. It is giving up. Feeling ourselves means feeling the inner energy which has carried us thus far in life.[31]

An interesting paper by Dragadze discusses the unusually late attribution of adulthood in the Caucasus republic of Georgia.[32] There the mediation between their own physical condition and the normative expectations of adulthood and old age can be problematic for some elderly people. In this society adult status is acquired in the late thirties and forties when people are considered to have acquired the level of self-restraint and wisdom to be regarded as responsible for their actions. Few words and much wisdom are what is expected. Elderly people who still retain good eyesight or hearing are likely to retain their full authority. Those people whose bodies do not function in ways necessary to compete fully in the economic and social life of the community respond by further withdrawal into more limited and isolated activities often outside the house, so that they can maintain the socially expected demonstration of self-control and carefully controlled comment and thus their adult status. Similarly social withdrawal by elderly people may be found in the Val d'Aosta but for different reasons. The social expectation of social equality there leads to strict rules of social reciprocity; for example, favours are always asked for, not offered. Thus elderly people who because of increasing infirmity are unable to offer reciprocal services and labour progressively isolate themselves socially.[33] The strategy of social withdrawal by elderly people does not appear to be common in Bosnia. The strong expectations both of family solidarity involving, if not joint living, continual mutual visiting, and the expectations of neighbourly help, which involve mutual exchange of visits for coffee, have a strong, socially integrating effect for elderly people. In these circumstances of expected sociability between extended kin and between neighbours, physical ability to maintain social activity and social status are related.

Understanding how people come to be allocated social roles and experience themselves and others on the basis of their age has been the theme of this chapter. Simplistic associations between chronological age and physical and social dependency need to be challenged. Even if the experience of a life cycle in which an individual feels a sense of loss when they have passed their 'prime' is a universal; it says nothing about the timing, meaning and cultural content of the social category of old age. The variety of ways of being 'old' are as different as the ways of being in one's 'prime'. A re-evaluation of old age in the West requires an appreciation of the variety of ways it is possible to live one's 'old age' and an escape from culturally bound stereotypes of a 'normal old age'.

Peter Laslett (1989) locates a cultural poverty in the contemporary experience of ageing which must be changed for the benefit of future generations.[34] Laslett's analysis sees the problem of the third age as a cultural one; thus there is a need, to which he devoted a great deal of time and energy, to develop and give meaning to the last third of life as a period of personal growth and development. He sees cultural change lagging behind demographic change. The ageing of populations, which has been identifiable in Britain at least since 1911, has expanded the older age groups in society, but Laslett suggests no new roles have developed to give social meaning to these enlarged groups. His approach locates the indignities of old age as the lack of cultural value, old age as a contentless role – the fag-end of life lacking the charisma of youth. Laslett brought his formidable historical expertise to the redefinition of the problem of old age, but his excellent historical demography must not lull us into the view that cultures are either inherently inflexible, or not closely tied into the social and demographic fabric of society. Any failure on the part of society to change its cultural evaluation of old age requires explanation just as much as any continuity in values. In a similar argument, Riley draws attention to what she sees as the failure of modern Western societies to provide suitable roles appropriate for the growing numbers of elderly people.[35] Social institutions and popular philosophy, she argues, have fallen behind technology and economic advance. Outmoded social institutions are failing to provide opportunities for the growing aspirations of increased numbers of older people. While superficially having merit, care is needed with this apparently common-sense point of view because it assumes social change follows an inevitable course. It is falsely assumed that there is an automatic process by which these social inadequacies are corrected, as ideas and social institutions 'catch up'. We need to ask what is perpetuating such adverse social and cultural conditions. Rather than 'outmoded institutions' being the problem, it is the construction of new structures of oppression and ageism that needs to be examined.

2

THE SUCCESSION OF GENERATIONS

The Ostler's daughter: My Gran was born at the end of the nineteenth century into a family of ostlers in rural Kent. She came to London as a child when her father came to look after the horses for Hansom Cabs. When I was a child I knew her as a large, kindly but strict woman and just what a gran should be – a wonderful cook who would produce enormous roast dinners, wonderful cakes, and whose Christmas Pudding (with silver threepenny pieces in) was out of this world. She lived to over ninety, outliving her husband by thirty years and two of her children. She retained her love of horses all her life, and although she would never, as a Methodist, gamble, she followed the horse racing on the afternoon television avidly.

SOCIAL GROUPS BASED ON AGE

Whatever the universality of ageing as a biological or a psychological phenomenon, different societies clearly use age as a basis for social cohesion and differentiation in a variety of ways. 'Old age' as a set of people may refer to either an age group or a generation. There are those who have a specific chronological age range in common. There are also people whose common experience lies in being born around the same time. The subjective experience for those currently in old age may be very similar. From a sociological point of view, the difference is important to understanding the dynamics of social change. Age and generation form different bases for social relationships and social cohesion.

Social groups can form on the basis of age. People move in and out of these groups as they grow older, but the age ranges and the social attributes of such age groups clearly vary greatly from society to society. Age is a continuum; age groups are formed when a specific age range is differentiated and takes on a social significance. In the modern West the social category 'teenager' is relatively new. Sociologists in the 1950s were concerned to explain this new social group. Eisenstadt discussed circumstances in which chronological age was likely to become a significant method of social solidarity.[1] He suggested that age groups tend to arise in those societies whose methods of social integration are mainly 'universalistic'. He understood the developing youth phenomenon in post-war America as meeting the need to facilitate the transition from family to work in modern society. He saw the increasing emphasis on age-group membership as a mechanism through which a sense of solidarity wider than the family could be internalised prior to leaving for the larger world of work.[2] Thus it has been argued that age-group solidarity enables teenagers to move from the particularistic milieu of the family towards the universalistic world of work with the minimum of social disruption. A similar mode of argument may be found in the functionalist role-stripping model of old age that was developed by Cummings and Henry.[3] They saw the transition from middle age to old age as requiring the stripping away of roles, for example, disengagement from work roles – the reverse of Eisenstadt's process of preparation for the world outside of the family. Stereotypes of the value of 'old age' are built into these ideas. These functionalist perspectives do not question the absence of equivalent age-group cultural mechanisms for the opposite transition to ease people out of 'universalistic' work roles back into domestic ones. Nor do they question ageist assumptions about the value and potential of old age.

WHAT DO WE MEAN BY GENERATION?

The term 'generation' is frequently used to mean 'cohort'. The term 'cohort' refers to sets of people who are born at the same time. By virtue of this common characteristic, they age simultaneously and consequently have many experiences in common. 'Generation' also has a number of alternative possible connotations, including successions of parents and children. For example, aristocrats, who boast of owning their estate since Charles II granted it to one of his illegitimate sons, call themselves the 'twelfth generation'. Similarly the term 'second-generation' immigrant is used to suggest that there are common social factors to being the child of an immigrant. Identifiable social groups can form on the basis of generation in the sense of cohort. Just as age is a continuous variable, so dates of birth can be allocated only to cohort categories by culturally constructed systems of classification. Such groups frequently coalesce around formative historical experiences and adopt distinctive cultural symbols. The sense of social solidarity, of belonging to a generation and developing a sense of fellow feeling with those of the same cohort, depends on at least two factors. The first is having a cultural system of classification that can allocate people into groups on the basis of birth order. The second is the process by which those who are classified together develop a sense of common identity.

Cohorts in some societies are part of the formal social structure. In tribal societies, institutions based on age can serve to cut across loyalties to specific kinship groups and enable larger numbers of people to co-ordinate their ritual or political activities than otherwise might be the case. For example, many of the pastoral tribes of East Africa have an age set structure. These age sets are cohorts identified through ritual initiation. Everyone initiated into manhood between one 'closing ceremony' and the next belongs to a common group. This group has a name, and members have specific rights and duties to each other as well as collectively to other such groups that are older and younger than themselves. These societies also tend to have formalised *age grades* into which successive age sets (cohorts) pass and which are the collection of social roles required of each group. So each formalised generation (age set) takes its turn at key functions in society (age grade), such as warrior, elder or ritual specialist.

Cohorts are also socially recognised in modern societies such as those of the industrialised West. In the previous chapter I discussed ways in which the bureaucratic and institutional structure of modern society uses age as a criterion of social differentiation. The definition of education, civic and military service, and work rights and duties by age tends to mean cohorts can develop a common sense of identity. This may take the form of class groups at school or college (the class of '47) or those who did their military service together and keep in touch and hold reunions. Changes in historical circumstance – age of conscription, age of education, as well as age-based institutional procedures – help establish the boundaries and communality of these generations. Those who grew up together during a certain historical period form a group that feels a sense of communality throughout their lives. The nature, age range and depth of communality are related to historical circumstances. Rapid change in society means that people with quite close dates of birth may well have distinct sets of experience; the social distance represented by the 'generation gap' needs to be examined and established empirically.[4]

GENERATION, COMMUNITY AND INEQUALITY

A particularly good view of the changing conditions of older people, especially those living at the more deprived end of the social spectrum, may be derived from the work of the research team of Phillipson, Bernard, Phillips and Ogg based at the University of Keele.[5] In the late 1990s they looked again at communities that had been studied in the 1950s in previous classic sociological research on older people. They studied communities that experience a high degree of deprivation and which were located in dense inner urban areas. Their findings tell us a lot about both the changes in British society over the past fifty years and the condition of old age.

The original studies were conducted in Wolverhampton, a Midlands industrial town (now a city); Bethnal Green, an inner-city area in the East End of London; and Woodford, a suburb on the borders of London and Essex. The Keele team found that there are some important continuities from the past and that, contrary to many common preconceptions, family and kinship remained strong. They suggest that kinship ties have stood up well to the developments affecting urban societies over the past fifty years. Their re-study was conducted in areas that previously had been found to have very strong family and kinship ties. The original studies found that older people defined their lives largely in the context of family groups. These relationships had changed but had done so in ways that are recognisable as common patterns elsewhere in Britain.[6] Most older people are connected to family-based networks which provide many different types of support. Although the incidence of multi-generational families living together had declined, crucially there are still mutual patterns of support within families and kin. In the 1950s, Townsend found that in Bethnal Green, a majority (54 per cent) of older people shared a dwelling with relatives, while in Wolverhampton in the 1940s, only 10 per cent of elderly people lived alone.[7] The pattern of older people living with their children may have been the result partly of the housing shortage following wartime destruction. However, the desire of both younger and older generations to retain their independence and avoid living in extended families does not indicate a failure of family relationships or an unwillingness to devote very significant time and resources to supporting family members.

Older people both give and receive support as it is needed. They expect to reciprocate assistance, but to do so in ways that are compatible with their abilities and resources. Kinship networks seem to have a central core that is the key focus in distributing help in a variety of ways. In the main part spouses, but also daughters, are the main providers of both emotional aid and practical support. The immediate family 'offers an important protective role to older people: reassuring in times of crisis, playing the role of confidant, and acting as the first port of call if help is needed in the home'.[8] The changes over the past fifty years have focused provision of support towards the immediate rather than the wider extended family. While a wider set of kin may come together for birthdays, weddings and anniversaries it does not necessarily represent a readily available source of emotional, practical or financial support. Indeed as people age, funerals start to outnumber weddings in the proportion of 'rites of passage' ceremonies attended and kin networks decline numerically. Phillipson *et al.* find that there is a selection of one or two close family members who provide significant support for dependent older people. Which individuals within a person's social network are selected to provide such support may be seen to form a pattern derived from negotiation. This pattern reflects the practicalities and obligations around not only emotional ties but also family histories of work, migration and other commitments.[9]

Changes in residential patterns for older people have gone hand in hand with changing patterns of family support. Wolverhampton as a large industrial town had a rather different experience from the metropolitan-based studies of inner-city Bethnal Green or suburban Woodford. There, compared to the other locations, the researchers felt that ties to kin and neighbours had undergone less fragmentation since the original study. Close kin were still available and significant in the lives and networks of older people. Relations with more distant kin were not necessarily sustained; for many families it was the grandmother's funeral that provided the last occasion when the cousins came together to socialise. Asked 'Who is important in your life?', 'Who provides you with support?', the majority of the Keele team's informants replied by referring to kin.[10] Nevertheless, there is a well-established trend that will have implications for ways in which it is possible to live a satisfactory old age. That is to say, we have moved from a world of kin to a world of friends, neighbours, leisure associates and kin.

In contemporary Britain, family life centres around husband and wife. Couples live together for long periods after the children have left home and provide the major source of emotional and physical care for each other into deep old age. Although the importance of family increases with age, social life centres around friends and leisure-based acquaintances with common interests. Phillipson's team and other research suggests that friends are the largest single group identified by informants as the locus of intimate ties in old age, and that for the single and widowed they play a substantial role in providing emotional support.[11] In their 1950s studies Young and Willmott emphasised the contrasting importance of extended family in (what we would now call inner-city) Bethnal Green with the 'symmetrical family' of more suburban Woodford.[12] Woodford illustrated a particularly modern form of social intimacy:

> Woodford respondents could be seen as examples of the 'dispersed extended family', where regular contact (weekly or more often) is maintained through the motor car and the telephone. On the one hand, this group appears as an exemplar of Rosenmayr and Kockeis' notion of 'intimacy at a distance', in some cases, pushing the logic of this attitude as far as it can possibly go. On the other hand, intimacy is maintained through enduring friendships, those representing long-standing members of older people's social convoy. In this regard, the world of the Woodford elderly is at least as much friendship- as kinship-based, a pattern which was laid down in the 1950s in the move to a suburban and largely middle-class world.[13]

Family demography may also play an important part in the relative decline of the extended family network. Smaller families mean fewer siblings, and thus fewer in-laws and, over time, fewer uncles, aunts and cousins. Completed family size declined from between 5.5 and 6 children per married woman in the 1850s to

2.2 in the 1930s, while women aged 30 in 1990 had an average of 1.42 children.[14] For some minority groups, particularly among British Asians, extended family and kinship remains a very strong factor in providing a different experience of old age. Even in these cases, however, it is important not to over-emphasise a stereotypical single experience. Many Asian elderly whose family networks have been broken by death, or forced migration as refugees or economic loss, may experience social isolation. Phillipson suggests in his Bethnal Green studies that the availability of support for minority elders seemed more problematic for people whose migration histories had broken up the continuity of their social relationships.[15]

The conditions in Bethnal Green found by Phillipson *et al*. seemed to be particularly difficult. They noted that continuing problems in retirement of boredom, poverty and missing contacts from work affected a substantial minority. The team identified some older people who seemed to have 'substantially withdrawn from what might be taken as a reasonable standard of daily life'.[16] In the original 1950s study carried out by Peter Townsend, he referred to these people as 'social isolates'.[17] They invariably lived alone and were disconnected in important ways from the community around them. In the 1990s, the Keele team found this pattern of living was still present. Phillipson *et al*. express concern that twenty-seven people in their study were unable to cite a single activity which was significant or important in their lives (eighteen of whom were drawn from their Bethnal Green sample). They specify that this group of isolated pensioners represented only 4 per cent of their total sample, but that they are present at all after fifty years of the welfare state must be a concern. These 'social isolates', although living in areas with substantial minority populations, were mainly (78 per cent) white. They were predominantly very elderly. The majority (56 per cent) were single and lived alone.[18]

This interplay between generations, and the way social and economic change influences family and kinship support in old age, was reflected in Bosnia. The changing relationship between urban industrial society and rural subsistence-agricultural society in Bosnia had consequences for elderly people. That part of the Balkans has a tradition of very large patrilineal extended families. However, geographical and occupational mobility, as well as urban living in flats, meant that it was difficult to sustain such extended family living in an industrial society. Although fragmentation occurred, there was more continuity in the rural areas. There, even if a joint household was not preserved, it was possible to build new houses on family land or construct separate apartments in different parts of a new large house such that the old people had their married children living in close proximity.

In Bosnia societal changes and family structures are different to urban Britain. However, changing social conditions there also inform us about changing networks and the social construction of loneliness and isolation. It is possible to distinguish three kinds of family situation common to rural Bosnia: first, where the extended household is still intact; second, where at least one child, usually a son and a daughter-in-law, live either in a separate section of the same house or in a neighbouring house; and third, the situation which is found in those villages that have seen a massive out-migration. In these communities much of the migration has been abroad and the old couple are left with only occasional holiday visits from their children. It is in this latter circumstance where the most difficult situations of social isolation for elderly people can occur. However, in the first and second types of household there are different kinds of problem. The elderly people whose children do not actually live with them can still feel lonely. They can still feel that their expectations of joint living have been let down, and can still experience grief at loss of spouses, kin, and friends and neighbours of the same generation. It is wrong to over-idealise extended family living as a position for elderly people. Extended families, like other forms of family, have their tensions and although daughters-in-law may do their duty, it is not necessarily the case that these relationships are without conflict.[19]

Phillipson *et al.* emphasise that it is misleading to stereotype older people and their social relationships. There is no single model of the family life of older people. He identifies an increasing diversity of family life for older people, reflecting complex patterns of urban change and migration histories based on different social class and intergenerational relations. Further a similar diversity is to be found in the kinds of communities in which older people are embedded. The different and largely separate lives of white and Bengali communities in Bethnal Green may be used to illustrate this point. The Bengali community is the largest minority group in the borough and has replaced the former East End Jewish community which, particularly in the pre-war years, faced similar hostile reactions from many 'white' residents. The Bengalis had many strong family ties, associated with traditions of extended family living adapted for the requirements of long-distance migration, but had weak links into the locality through neighbours and locality networks. Phillipson *et al.* suggest that in some respects white elderly people in Bethnal Green have become 'network poor'.[20] Their white respondents are isolated in the sense of having lost their traditional network kin and neighbours without having a clear replacement. Although there are modern forms of neighbourliness and community involvement, and perhaps particularly for the retired population, for many in Bethnal Green and other inner-city localities this is largely unrealised. Fear of crime and especially the suspicion and alienation existing between white and Bengali residents prevents many cohesive networks from emerging.[21]

THE CHANGING EXPERIENCE OF DIFFERENT HISTORICAL COHORTS

The experience of family and community in old age differs across Britain but it also differs across generations. In the flow of successive cohorts, each lives through a unique segment of historical time and confronts its own particular sequence of social and environmental events and changes. Society changes, and therefore people in different cohorts age in different ways. People in Britain who were children in the First World War, were starting families in the Great Depression of the 1930s, went through the Second World War in prime middle age, and reached retirement when the long post-war economic boom was coming to an end, had one experience of old age. The cohort born in the post-war baby boom who as teenagers and young adults experienced the changes in social conventions of the 1960s, and the collective sense of liberation at that time, has consequently a degree of common identity as 'baby boomers', and will have another experience of old age. The ageing process itself is altered by social change.[22] How distinctive old age is felt to be from other times of life depends significantly on the experience of cohort.

There is a small but growing body of research that demonstrates the significance of differing cohort experiences in contemporary society. An excellent French study by Françoise Cribier demonstrates how relatively short age spans with quite chronologically close dates of birth can have very significantly different life experiences.[23] She analysed the results of two longitudinal studies based on interviews with large representative samples of people from Greater Paris. The two cohorts studied were those who first drew their pensions in 1972 and 1984. The traumatic events of the First World War divided the dates of birth of the older cohort (1906–12) from the younger cohort (1919–24). The retirement of these groups can be dated as 1972 for the older and 1984 for the younger, and they were interviewed three years later in 1975 and 1987 respectively.

There were educational contrasts between the two groups. The older cohort left school around 1920, while the younger benefited from advances made in French schooling in the inter-war period. Between the two cohorts the proportion of retired people without any qualifications decreased from 40 per cent to 20 per cent among men and from 48 per cent to 27 per cent among women. The older cohort had reached age 25 by the time of the severe economic crisis in 1932 which had consequences for their work careers. On the other hand, the younger cohort reached age 25 in 1947 at the beginning of twenty-five years of sustained economic growth. Low-skilled work and low-qualified employees constituted half of the newly retired population 1972 but only one-third in 1984.[24]

In terms of family, the older group brought up their children in the 1930s and during the Second World War, without family allowance or social housing. The younger groups were more fortunate. Their children grew up after the war, when French social policy favoured the family. In terms of family size, the results may be counter-intuitive but are very revealing. Thirty per cent of men in the older cohort (who had children) had three or more, while for the younger cohort the figure was 42 per cent. In other words the younger cohort was more likely to have the larger family of procreation. The median age of the respondent at the birth of their last child was the same for both cohorts at 31 (i.e. half the families were completed by that age). However, the age dispersions among the younger cohort were smaller; they had their children closer together.[25] The younger cohort planned their families and experienced less disruption to their family development than did the older group.

People are now living longer, so the 1984 retirees were more likely to have elderly parents alive. The proportion of those who had at least one parent or parent-in-law alive at retirement increased from 11 per cent for the older cohort in 1975 to 26 per cent for the younger cohort in 1987. However, the extended family has declined for the French as it has for the British. The proportion of persons living with their spouse and only the spouse rose from 62 per cent to 68 per cent for men and from 35 per cent to 40 per cent for women. There was a greater chance of having parents alive when they retired but less desire to live with them. The family, as simply the conjugal couple, became stronger with the younger cohort. Where multi-generation families existed these were often associated with problematic achievement of life transitions. Among these 75- to 80-year-olds who still had children living with them fourteen years after their retirement in 1986, in one out of four cases the child was likely to be handicapped.[26]

Only 27 per cent of the older cohort had had a father who had experienced retirement, while for the younger cohort the proportion was about 50 per cent. Expectations of retirement on a pension were different between the quite narrow age ranges represented by the two groups. Not surprisingly, given their better education and work opportunities and the progress of the welfare state, there was an average of 20 per cent difference in pension on retirement. The younger cohort not only had retirement incomes one-fifth higher, they were also able to retire earlier – 66 per cent of the older cohort and 36 per cent of the younger cohort took their pension at age 65 or older. The social geography of Paris is represented in the different cohort experiences. In the younger cohort only 25 per cent lived in central Paris on retirement as opposed to 36 per cent of the older cohort. A further contrast found 40 per cent of the 1984 retirees living in the outer suburbs while only 28 per cent of the older group lived there.[27] This pattern was also indicated in London by the contrasts between Bethnal Green and Woodford documented by Phillipson's team.

Cribier's study reveals the dramatically different life experiences of those in old age at the last part of the twentieth century. Old people are not all the same; they differ significantly from each other on the basis of birth cohort. The influence of generational experience – educational, familial, economic and locational differences structure the possibilities of old age. The experiences described by Cribier, although specific to Paris, could be mirrored in metropolitan areas all across Western Europe. Even though there was only eleven years' average age difference between the cohorts she describes, the possibilities in old age for those born in the period after the First World War were greatly enhanced by the relative peace and prosperity they experienced throughout their adult lives and this is reflected in their attitudes to retirement:

In 1975 many of those who had had to cease working before age 65 explained that they were not lazy, but could not find any work or were too worn out to continue working. By 1987 it was those who worked up until the age of 64–65 who justified themselves, explaining that they were not 'stealing jobs' but that they needed the salary, that they had to complete their insurance record or that their employers needed them. Only senior executives did not feel the need to justify themselves in this way.[28]

The preceding analysis suggests the importance of generation as a source of differentiation. It shows that important elements of class and community stem from the historical experience of cohorts as they age. Each cohort carries embedded features of history that structure where and how people live, their occupational opportunities and their sense of solidarity. It can similarly be demonstrated that generation impacts on all the other major categories of social differentiation, including gender, ethnicity and sexuality. Jane Pilcher has done an excellent empirical study of the attitudes of women of three related generations.[29] Her topic of interest was feminism and how grandmothers, daughters and granddaughters thought about feminism and a range of issues that are important to feminists. Her research tool was in-depth qualitative interviews and she is able to illustrate how different generations hold contrasting sets of values and attitudes related to issues about employment, domestic life and sexuality. The concerns and priorities of younger feminists were not necessarily those of older women. The point she is able to demonstrate clearly is the integration of values and attitudes and the interpretation of experience. Although there was a range of attitudes within each generation she found clear generational differences. For example, the changes in attitudes to sex divided cohorts who developed their attitudes prior to or after the 1960s.

Generation also impacts on the processes of ethnic differentiation. In debates about ethnicity and race (these terms being used somewhat differently in Britain than in the USA), there have been considerable shifts in the extent to which generation has been considered relevant. To the extent that such debates have been framed in terms of migration, sequential differences in the experiences of different waves of migrants and settlers have been considered to be important. For example, use of the terms first, second and third generation to describe members of ethnic groups indicates a social dynamic. What was problematic about such formulations, particularly functionalist formulations of the 1950s and 1960s, was that they took the perspective of the dominant culture. The trajectory across generations was assumed to be assimilation. Such views underplayed issues to do with the dominant or host society, most importantly cultural and institutional racism. Hence generational issues have become downplayed within the sociology of race relations. However, with the cultural turn in sociology and greater participation by minority social scientists in documenting the diversity of multi-ethnic societies, issues of generation are again being revealed. This occurs in a number of ways. One of these is through the documentation of new and vibrant hybrid, Creole cultures expressed through music, literature, fashion, cuisine and much else, which form part of the youth element of generational change. Another is the ageing of the black minorities who came to Britain in the 1950s and 1960s and the realisation among suppliers of health and social care that research is needed if serious attempts are to be made to provide equality of provision for minority elders. The differentiation by generation of groups within the societies receiving migrants is mirrored in the differentiation, including issues of generation, in the sending communities. In Chapter 3 issues of migration in the context of globalisation will be considered further.

Sexuality is a further area of diversity which has become increasingly articulated and which is also reflected in the development of specific, largely cultural sociologies. Gay and lesbian experience of ageing is part of these studies and can also inform and demonstrate the importance of understanding generational processes. In a fascinating paper, Dana Rosenfeld has documented the impact of social change on the way lesbian and gay people work at their identity.[30] She demonstrates significant changes, indeed almost a reversal, in the strategies different generations use to present and explain themselves to different audiences. She identifies pre- and post-Stonewall generations, those who established their homosexual identity before and after the successful establishment of a social movement around gay pride and gay rights. The former evolved strategies for dealing with their homosexuality as a 'discreditable' identity while the latter were concerned to validate their identities as legitimately 'accredited' homosexuals.

> The discreditable identity cohort sees its goal not as avoiding enacting homosexuality, but enacting it only in the presence of homosexuals while 'passing' in the company of heterosexuals. . . . For the accredited, the goal was not to pass as heterosexual, but to achieve authentic relations with self and (homosexual and heterosexual) others, a project that centered on disclosing one's homosexuality to others when it become relevant.[31]

Thus generation is an important and insufficiently understood source of social diversity. In some circumstances these differences drive people apart into age-segregated social groups. In others they are seen as a valuable source of social change and cultural diversity to be celebrated. Differences in experience do make it difficult for people to understand and sympathise with the predicament of those from different generations. On the other hand, the rich diversity of experience should be a resource for wisdom in old age and one that society recognises and values. However, diversity between generations does not mean that they are socially isolated from each other. Each generation mutually affects the ways it is possible for other generations to live out their lives.

THE INTERACTION OF GENERATIONAL EXPECTATIONS

There are complex and dynamic patterns by which the life courses of different cohorts affect one another. Cohort differences in ageing are socially dynamic because any major changes affecting one cohort have consequences for the next and subsequent cohorts. Declines in mortality rates and changes in the standard of living, education, childbearing and health affecting cohorts across this century have structured the circumstances of succeeding cohorts. A century ago over three-quarters of a cohort died before reaching adulthood, today over three-quarters of a cohort survive to at least age 65 and increasing proportions make it to age 85. The consequences of this increased longevity are various and complex. It allows education to be prolonged, and perhaps this is one reason why each successive cohort has experienced certificate inflation whereby the certification required to gain access rights to a job or profession is higher for each succeeding generation. Changes in family role relationships in one cohort produce implications for kinship in successive cohorts. Among couples marrying a century ago in America, one or both partners were likely to have died before the children were grown up; today (if not divorced) they can anticipate surviving together for an average of forty to fifty years. Today parents and children share a longer period of their lives as adult age-status equals than they do as adult and dependent child. In 1900 more than half of middle-aged couples had no surviving elderly parents, while today half have two or more parents still alive. Hence the grandparents in current cohorts born post-Second World War are able to have more influence on the lives of their grandchildren than those born a hundred years before.

In the twentieth century there have been major changes in the division of labour, and work rights are frequently associated with retirement possibilities. There have been sequential alterations in work lives of successive cohorts of older people. For example, one trend, particularly in the past fifty years, has been increasing numbers and proportions of professional workers. The uniqueness, power, status and rewards of professional occupations have changed. Access to professional work is achieved through prolonged periods of education and training with an emphasis on certification. Changing cohort opportunities for professional work are related to extending periods of education and differential access to education for many. Thus there are different opportunity structures between and within cohorts in terms of access to the top professional jobs. The changing life course associated with a professionalisation of the workforce has thus had different consequences for successive cohorts. The social consequences extend into old age. Better educated elderly people with a history of professional employment and occupational pensions can live a different old age from those in manual employment with little education and basic pensions. Members of each cohort's response to social change exert a collective force for further change as they move through the age-stratified society. The increased numbers of professionals in the ranks of the retired can produce articulate pensioner pressure groups which resist exclusion from social life and thus change old age. They can also fracture the class solidarity as the foundation of pension and trade union action to secure collective benefits for state pensioners.[32]

Members of the cohort who were born in the years 1920 to 1930 have had opportunities achieved by the struggles of the preceding generation for universal retirement pensions. They retired with greater security than their parents. This same cohort has been affected by the increasing proclivity of their children to separate and divorce. Thus they may be obstructed in meeting their expectations of grandparenthood. The life chances of one cohort have been determined in part by the actions of immediately preceding and succeeding cohorts. In family life there have been increases in divorce and remarriage that, combined with increasing longevity in modern cohorts, convert the current kinship structure into a complex matrix of latent relationships among dispersed kin and step-kin among whom ties of solidarity must be achieved rather than taken for granted.[33]

Society, therefore, is not only composed of successive cohorts of individuals who are themselves ageing in new ways, but these cohorts have a continuing impact on other cohorts, requiring them to make adjustments to their social roles. As one cohort presses for adjustments in social roles and social values, they influence other people throughout the age strata and contribute to continuing interaction in both ageing and social structure.[34]

GENERATIONS AND SOCIAL CHANGE

Age and generation – the experience of ageing and the experience of history – intersect and form their own dynamic. The human life span sets a rhythm to the succession into sequential age roles across the life course and the inevitable succession of generations, but social change has no such inbuilt rhythm. Social change can be slow, fast, revolutionary, or even unnoticed or denied. The divergence between the pace of historical change and the rhythm of succeeding generations itself creates a dynamic for change. For example, the younger generation in Africa in the final twenty years of the twentieth century saw their parental generation experience rapid and long-range social mobility following decolonialisation. This long-range social mobility of their parents created expectations for their own advancement. However, the recent history of population growth and economic stagnation has frustrated many of these expectations held by younger Africans. This frustration has been a force for both instability and change in Africa.[35]

Another potentially fruitful way of looking at the relationship between generational change and historical patterns of social interaction derives from the work of Norbert Elias. Elias sought to demonstrate the way personality structures have changed in the context of historically changing patterns of social inter-action. Elias is probably most well known in Britain for his work *The Civilising Process*.[36] This is a classic work of historical sociology in which he seeks to demonstrate how the centralisation of power in fewer and fewer states in Western Europe led to the development of manners and the internalisation of controlled and restrained behaviour. The change was from the temper of a warrior, willing and able to 'summon up the blood' and personally engage in mortal combat, to that of a courtier skilled at the charm, mannerisms and intrigue necessary for success in courtly society. The specifics of the historical detail of this part of Elias' work are extremely useful in understanding the repugnance with which old age is held. He demonstrates the ways in which control of bodily functions in public has a developing history, becoming part of 'good manners' and then became internalised into our personalities. Thus failure to show appropriate bodily self-restraint – urinating, dribbling, inability to present an attractive appearance – results in a sense of shame and failure on the part of the individual and a feeling of revulsion in others. This has clear implications for understanding the ageing body. In his much less well-known work *The Loneliness of the Dying*, Elias specifically tackles the social condition of old age.[37] He based his approach on the overall themes of his life's work – interconnectedness and the way individuals are embedded in historically derived social networks. As the embeddedness of older people becomes less, the effect is an increased sense of isolation and loneliness. From Elias' perspective it is not the cultural evaluation of the social function of old age that is critical but rather control and use of the body which comes to determine social status in old age. This is a theme picked up later in this book in Chapter 6. Elias argues that the detachment from networks which give validation to the individual's sense of self and self-worth is a key problem and he links this to approaching death. The absence of future anticipated social relations loosens people from the mutual exchanges that form the core of social life. His demonstration of the working through of long chains of historical interconnectedness linking macro-institutional features to internalised personality structures needs greater attention as a means of understanding generational succession. His concept of 'figurations' is one way in which one can look at historical experiences of cohorts and the mutual influence of successive cohorts on each other and understand how these large-scale features of society and history are also intimate and personal aspects of each individual.

THE SOCIAL SOLIDARITY OF GENERATIONS

Analytically there are two processes of social integration going on simultaneously. There are those processes which cut across generations and link people together in family, kinship and community groups, and there are those which link them together with people in cohorts and differentiate them from people of other generations. Using the label 'generation' for a cohort emphasises the cross-cutting ties between cohorts by referring to the image of the family, the family being made up of multiple 'generations'. To develop a distinctive identity a generation needs to have a symbolic repertoire that enables it to differentiate itself from other cohorts. A key issue in understanding the formation of generations is to identify the circumstances in which specific cohorts come to attract social definition, how they acquire a name, a symbolic unity, and a definition of the birth dates they cover.

Relationships between generations should also be looked at through the framework of conflict sociology. This perspective emphasises that the dynamic for historical changes stems from conflicts of interest between social groups and the outcome of the struggles that ensue. This is a very useful approach to dissecting the roots of historical social change. In some ways generations are similar to classes but different in many other ways. This is one theme of Mannheim's work.[38] Classes by definition have common economic interests and they frequently develop an awareness of this common position. As a result classes may act collectively in pursuit of their common interests. There is a very large amount of sociological literature that has examined how historically some classes have developed a stronger sense of cohesion and solidarity than others. There is much less socio-logical examination of generations as social movements. It is relatively easy to generate a cultural sociology of generations, one that examines the symbolic construction of identity. It is much less easy to be able to demonstrate the social consequences of cohorts developing common material interests. However, common historical experiences may lead a generation to have more than simply a common sense of identity but also to develop collective economic interests. When this happens generations may take on a greater class-like character and it becomes possible to see more clearly their role in social conflict and social change. For example, in Britain, historical changes in housing and property ownership have given people of different generations different entitlements and assets. The generation reaching retirement in the 1990s was the first in which a substantial proportion had property rights derived from a lifetime of paying a mortgage. The tax-based subsidies for property ownership and enormous inflation in house prices have created generationally based conflicts of interest between property-owning generations and those property-less generations newly creating households who are substantially disadvantaged in obtaining accommodation. Conflicts have also arisen between the rights of property-owning generations over claims from the state to realise those property assets to pay for residential care in old age, a service that formerly was available free from the state. However, there is little sign that such generationally based conflicts are, in Britain, manifesting themselves in formal political arenas, but they clearly have profound implications for the well-being of different sections of British society.[39]

It is clear that some historical circumstances can create divergences of interest between different generations. Viewing inequality from a life-course perspective draws attention to both on the one hand large-scale historical social movements and, on the other, to people's whole life experience rather than their current social category. Such an approach can make a significant contribution to the understanding of inequality in old age. Studies of inequality based simply on cultural criteria tend to be static. We can look at the cultural symbols through which people come to identify with a generation. But to understand the extent to which older people are a cohesive social group, a class with common interests or fragmented along the same lines as the rest of society requires an examination of social conflict. It is argued that the size of the post-war generation and the structure of the welfare state has produced a situation which has placed generations in conflict with one another. This will be the subject of Chapters 3 and 4.

3

GLOBAL CRISES AND OLD AGE

The Wrong Side of the Tracks: In Northern Bosnia we drove out of town past the factories, alongside the railway, until the houses petered out, then turned across an unmarked level crossing and down a track. A group of children indicated an old run-down cottage, a shack made of wood and mud. We held our breath at the stench of urine in the one-room hovel, empty except for a bed and a wood stove. Ivana was thin and frail, did not talk very much, she had problems with her memory. Her son lived in the farmhouse across a patch of land covered with odd bits of rusting machinery. The daughter-in-law sent across porridge. While we spoke, some four- or five-year-olds looked in the open door and shouted a few rude names at her. All she had was the rags on the bed, what she wore, some fragile family relationships and rapidly fading memories.

WHAT IS GLOBALISATION, HOW MIGHT IT IMPACT ON OLD AGE?

A proper study of old age requires an understanding of the possibilities of life in old age across the whole world and not merely those of people in the developed West. Opportunities for a prosperous, respected and healthy old age need to be constructed not only at local and national levels but also on a global level. There are a series of crises that can be seen to threaten global society and create problems for older people. Three important crises that are particularly relevant to the conditions of older people are those of poverty, population and environment.

- Globalisation and poverty are interrelated. What are the economic impacts of globalisation for different groups of older people? These impacts include not only the distribution of wealth but also migration and the redistribution of people around the world. What are the consequences of migration for older people?
- There have been various demographic crises identified. Rapid growth in world population is identified as one such crisis. The ageing of populations across the globe is presented as another. Are these demographic threats real?
- The world is also seen to be under threat from a variety of human-induced changes to the global environment – global warming, depletion of the ozone layer and spreading and accumulating pollutants are but three such threats. What is the relationship between old age and these environmental crises?

Globalisation seems to be a common factor in all three of these problem areas. It is a complex phenomenon with a variety of components and indeed many would argue that it is not a single phenomenon.[1] However, globalisation has been linked to social changes with impacts in all nations including aspects of communications, finance and capital, trade and industry, cultural pluralism, environment, health, disease and pollution. Communication of goods, people and information has become faster, cheaper and is conducted in ever-increasing volumes. Long-distance trade has a venerable history, but the extent of it on a global scale, and the extent to which local markets have to accommodate themselves to global markets are unprecedented. Knowledge of the world, and religious and political ideas and institutions, are much more freely available with profound social and cultural consequences, not least in the undermining of tradition as an authority for knowledge. In a global environment the common health of humanity depends on absence of pollution and disease throughout the world.

OLDER PEOPLE AND POVERTY

Poverty is the greatest obstacle to a secure old age in most of the world. With the possible exceptions of a few Scandinavian countries, older people feature significantly in the poorer sections of all societies. The United Nations Development Programme has estimated that only 20 per cent of people aged 60 or over in the world can be regarded as having income security. Retirement pensions are available to only a small proportion of the world's older people. Only 30 per cent of people aged 60 and over world-wide are eligible for any form of pension and most of these live in more developed countries. Pensions are most frequently the prerogative of those who work for government or for the formal sector of the economy; even in many quite highly developed countries the rural population has little or no cover. This does not necessarily mean that older people always become dependent on the support of families or others. Older people develop a variety of strategies for earning a living, for themselves and in support of their families. Many older people across the world continue to work for as long as they are physically able.

How does globalisation affect the unequal distribution of the benefits and disadvantages of old age? The political economy of later life is well developed in the social gerontological liter-ature. We can use it to acquire an understanding of the social and cultural consequences of the worldwide division of labour. The impact of globalisation on older people may be examined by asking: How is the division of labour organised? Who gains from the way the division of labour is organised? We can use this framework to ask about the specific position of older people compared to other social groups in the global economy and about how older people fit into the structure of competing interests which make up modern world society.

The first question is about the social relationships that enable society to organise production and create wealth – the division of labour. The division of labour is organised on an increasingly global scale – different parts of the world specialising in different kinds of production and different groups of people playing the constituent roles in the total process. This production is co-ordinated through global markets and global enterprises. Who has access to and who is excluded from the world market in labour? At the front of the queue are well-qualified professionals frequently from the West, near the back are unskilled workers from the Third World. This is demonstrated by the growing crisis in attempts to police international labour markets with more and more draconian anti-immigration measures. The poorest older people are those left behind by labour migration in the rural Third World, unsupported either by state welfare or attenuated kinship ties. As the spread of markets undermines divisions of labour based on the family, older people's social position is weakened.

In a society structured around the labour market, if most older people are retired or are excluded from access to paid work, they will be in a relatively weak and dependent position. This insight should not be taken to mean that older people do not engage in productive work. A variety of studies by HelpAge International and others suggest that the work undertaken by older people may be a paid job in the formal sector, but for many it may also include childcare, agriculture, trading, and other informal and sometimes unpaid duties. They estimate that half the world's older people are entirely reliant on informal livelihood arrangements. As a result, older people's contribution to their communities and societies is often not recorded in official statistics. Older people often make important contributions to their families; for example, domestic help can free up the time of other relatives to earn an income for the family.[2] While some older people are cared for by relatives, for many families poverty and other commitments, including the need to work, make this difficult. Older people strive for reciprocity and make contributions to the family as well, whether through earning a wage or assisting with childcare or agricultural work. Some older people have no relatives living with them at all, and are entirely responsible for their own livelihood. The pressures on older people to support themselves are increasing.[3] However, old people remain a significant part of the household economy and contribute to the domestic division of labour that produces benefits for those who live together in households and family groups. Those providing care for older people are usually their similarly elderly spouses. However, it is clear in our modern capitalist society that for most people it is paid work that gives access to money and status.

We can ask how the benefits of the new worldwide division of labour are redistributed globally. The way people are integrated to the market is key to such redistributions. Markets tend to have the effect of increasing differentiation. The rich and powerful tend to be able to make them work to their benefit. Those excluded from markets, perhaps by old age, tend to do less well. For example, modern society has defeated many of the causes of premature death, but medical care is subject to the global market. In the West, healthcare is characterised as becoming increasingly expensive. Hence pressures to ration healthcare by price or age. The greatest gains in life expectancy at the cheapest cost are to be made in the developing world, but in global terms healthcare is rationed by price, and older people in these countries are those least likely to receive modern healthcare. The globalised market in doctors, medicines and healthcare produces benefits for those with market clout.

An efficient global division of labour may produce wealth, but answers to the question about how the benefits of globalisation are distributed are socially complex. Much of the complexity stems from the enormous fragmentation of the division of labour in modern societies and the diversity of channels through which surplus value flows. Some redistributions may be seen as exploitative – people getting more than their fair share of society's rewards. Some may be seen as a legitimate insurance mechanism – an institutional arrangement to share life's risks. Mechanisms by which benefits are redistributed between age groups include transfers organised by the state. These include National Insurance contributions and tax revenue used for pay-as-you-go pension schemes and tax returns paid out as interest on national debt to bond-holding pension funds. Redistribution is also organised through commercial finance and investment markets in the form of dividends paid to private pension funds. Both of these mechanisms ensure that some older people benefit indirectly from the work of others. Much research has been done on the intergenerational redistribution within the family and via national pension schemes; less is known about other forms of redistribution. The social relationships of consumption also structure access to social production. Consumers have choice but do not come to the marketplace in an equal position to choose. Old age can result in a diminished ability to make the market work in one's favour: for example, through the limited availability of credit and the need of retired people to run down their savings; the small size of older households; problems with physical access to shopping; and difficulty with the use of modern consumer technologies. It is far from evident that older people are either exploiting younger people in the sense of living from their labour, or that middle-aged people's high average incomes represent a just distribution of the collective benefits of social production.

One difficulty in getting a clear-cut answer to this question about the distribution of the benefits of globalised production lies in how to calculate what counts as a benefit and in recognising dis-benefits. Concentrations of political and market power in the West tend to export economic risk to the developing world. The consequences of risks are becoming increasingly global.[4] Advocates of the 'too many old people, too few workers' argument still support a 'fortress Europe' to keep out young migrant workers. However, labour-market insecurities are as a consequence exported to the developing world where the old are most at risk. Indeed the global market in labour has considerable consequences in the movement of people and the well-being of older people.

Migration and the distribution of people around the world

The processes of globalisation have redistributed people around the world. They have moved people from countryside to town, from country to country and across continents. People have moved in vast numbers to seek new economic opportunities. Others have been forcefully evicted from the places of origin not only by poverty but by war, famine, expropriation and ethnic cleansing. Population ageing, social exclusion and poverty of older people are embedded in the relationships between migrants and their communities of origin and destination. Historically, what has been labelled 'development' has been associated primarily with young cities and not the 'traditional' countryside. Economic migrants are most likely to be young people, particularly those yet to start families. In many areas of the developing world, particularly in Asia, it is the men who are likely to leave to find new opportunities. Cities act as dynamic centres of modernity, offer expanding employment opportunities and are cultural centres for innovation and change. Older people with established ties, familial duties or who own or have rights in property are more likely to stay where they are and maintain a rural way of life.

The industrialisation and urbanisation of Europe and North America has been associated with rural depopulation and an ageing population in the countryside. However, here the decline in agricultural occupations has gone so far that many former areas with older populations are now experiencing rejuvenation as transport and communication systems mean that rural living becomes a more attractive option for families with non-agricultural occupations. In Bosnia in the rural areas there is considerable poverty concentrated among old people. Local people there did not define the problems of older people as different from those of everyone else – the need to keep body and soul together and to raise enough food and gain an income – problems which were the consequences of an overall low standard of living. However, this view stems from the mentality of a collective multi-generational household. In practice it was most difficult for older people to achieve those ends; younger people could more easily leave to find work. The economic problems for people in Bosnian towns are seen to be rather different. Those who had worked for industrial and commercial enterprises received pensions. Those older people who got a good pension were clearly substantially better off than those living in the country. However, this relative affluence was tempered by continuing problems of economic dependency. The pension did not prove to be reliable; it was not paid regularly, nor was it effectively cushioned against inflation in the economic and political chaos of a collapsing Yugoslavia. This experience of balancing support from families and from formal institutions is a continuing dilemma for old people across the developed and underdeveloped world.

International migration frequently follows a pattern known as chain migration. This pattern is built around continuing family and community ties between migrants and their home communities. Young single people tend to move first, to explore the possibilities in the new country. As they establish themselves successfully they provide assistance for further migrants to locate with them. Some migrants may return home but many create families in the cities and towns of the host nation. Although many migrants aspire to retire to their home village, many never do. Frequently the migrants will maintain links with home by sending money and attempting to keep up relationships with kin and community. Less often, once the migrants are successfully established in the new environment they will send home for the older generation to join them. Family re-creation and the arrival of older family members can have important consequences for ethnic identity and group formation.[5]

Transnational migration and rural–urban migration in general has a number of implications for old age. Frequently rural populations are old, and growing older. The older population without successors have much less incentive to invest and improve their farms. There are also important implications for relationships between generations and care of older people. Rural depopulation can also have environmental consequences. In some densely populated regions there may be some beneficial changes, created through reductions in intensive agriculture and soil erosion. In other areas there may be some detrimental consequences as the viability of agricultural support institutions such as those for irrigation and water-course management are undermined. The social conditions of those left behind in the migration can be adversely affected by the disruption of kinship obligations, and the social support across the generations. Those left behind, living at subsistence level in rural areas, are frequently the poorest people in a country. In much of the world, pensions and social welfare infrastructure tend to be urban-based and linked to formal employment. When those who depend on familial support for welfare in old age are left isolated by migration they can become extremely vulnerable. On the other hand, successful migrants who return from the city bringing newly acquired wealth, education and skills can have a positive effect on village life. Experience in a number of European countries suggests that local towns with better physical amenities are used as retirement locations rather than more isolated villages. Studies highlight the importance of social networks disrupted by migration, poverty and family breakdown for the quality of life of urban older people. Neglect of the interests of older people can in some instances be seen as stemming from incorporating the category 'rural' into the paradigm that equates tradition, old age and backwardness and from giving priority to urban development.

Although the proportions of older people are not high in the urban environments of the Third World or for migrants from the developing world to Europe and America, they can have specific identifiable problems that stem from migration and old age. Lloyd-Sherlock conducted an in-depth examination of the problems of older people in the shanty towns of Buenos Aires.[6] He identified problems of poverty, exacerbated by inadequacies of the pension schemes, fear of crime, lack of social cohesion and limits on self-organised help embedded in political repression.

In Africa and the Caribbean, young children are sometimes left behind in the care of rural grandparents. Where there is a high incidence of HIV/AIDS, older people are often responsible for the care of sick relatives or orphaned children. The vital role of the minimal state pension in sustaining older people in the townships around Cape Town and how this resource gets spread into the community is the subject of insightful studies by Sagner and Mtati.[7] Opportunities for self-provisioning in later life may become increasingly important if economic and family dislocation in the developing world continues to increase. Lloyd-Sherlock, for example, found that low-income elders in Argentinian and Brazilian cities usually had no steady sources of income but fell back on a variety of income strategies. They claimed a variety of small public benefits if they could prove they were eligible, took charity when they could, worked at informal or formal casual jobs and were helped by relatives and neighbours.[8]

Migration can affect older men and women differently. The ways in which women as opposed to men are attached to their localities, communities and families can differ. In many places the restriction of women to the domestic sphere means they have less tendency to migrate. The men travel to seek work and opportunities while the women remain at home. In some other situations, exclusive male ownership of land ties them to their local assets while the young women seek employment in town or overseas. Histories of relocation and dislocation can therefore affect men and women differently. In many island communities in the Caribbean region, there is a strong tradition of women-centred families. This has been related to a variety of historical and socio-cultural features, slavery, lack of economic opportunities, male seasonal and migrant labour. One consequence is the prevalence of grandmothers looking after their daughters' children, and a tendency for rural smallholdings to remain in the hands of older women. In contrast in poorer rural regions of the European periphery, for example, the rural west of Ireland, there has been a long-standing history of emigration, leaving a single male inheriting the farm who in many cases remains unmarried. Both of these examples illustrate how gender-based life courses create specific problems in later life for those 'left behind'.

Gail Wilson discusses the impact of globalisation on older people.[9] She asks how the relations between states and markets, between paid and unpaid work and between young and old and men and women affect the position of elders. She suggests that these changes make life easier and are, on balance, beneficial to elders in countries where pensions are adequate, but they lead to increased poverty and marginalisation when pensions are low. She argues cogently that globalisation and in particular the spread of market forces have highly differential impacts and older people cannot all share in the general improvements. They are exacerbated, for example, where there are significantly different consequences for men and women. There is a general tendency for markets to produce inequalities. Older people's status, prestige and access to resources are likely to be based on other social institutions than the market, and family and community are obvious examples. Older people have little market power, so that as market-based allocation of resources comes to predominate through globalisation, so older people lose out. Further, there are costs associated with the loss of community which result from the spread of market-based relationships; these costs are frequently borne by older people.

OLD AGE: POPULATION AND ENVIRONMENTAL CRISES

Population changes have frequently been seen as potential crises. However, the nature of these crises is constructed in a variety of ways. Third World population growth rates have been seen as a 'time bomb' – threatening over-population. In the 1950s and 1960s the over-population threat was seen largely as an inhibition to development and economic growth. However, it could be argued that the dramatic growth in world population has been the driving force for massive economic growth. Increasing numbers of jobs have been created to satisfy more and more consumers, and producers have been able to increase productivity through the economies of scale with larger and larger markets. More recently concerns have focused more on the environmental consequences of massive population growth, not only in terms of destruction of habitat to make way for increased human activity but by the realisation that if all countries industrialised 'successfully' the consequent resource depletion and pollution would threaten the sustainability of 'spaceship Earth'. Ironically, there are two kinds of population changes identified as crises, sometimes simultaneously. They are, first, too many young people – rapid increase in the birth rate and a global rise in population; and, second, too many old people – an increase in the average age of the world's population (Figure 3.1).

Population pyramids are the standard way of presenting diagrams of population. They show the relative size of age groups with the youngest at the bottom. The pyramids in Figure 3.2 are constructed with five-year age groups. The size of male groups

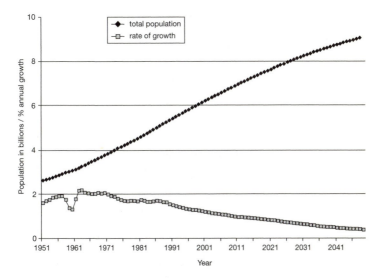

Figure 3.1 Growth of world population 1950 to 2050.
Source: Author's chart using data from US Census Bureau, International Data Base.

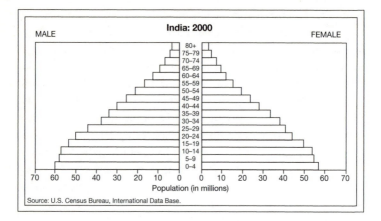

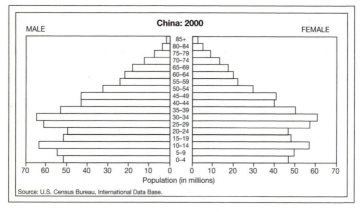

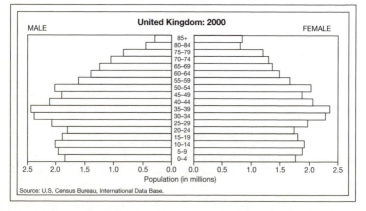

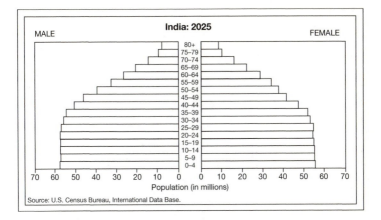

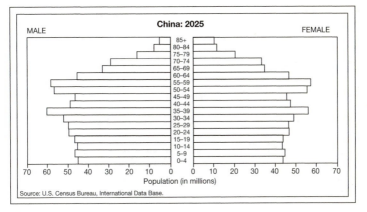

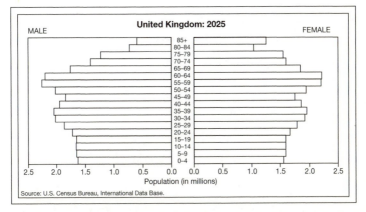

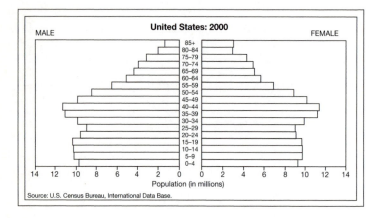

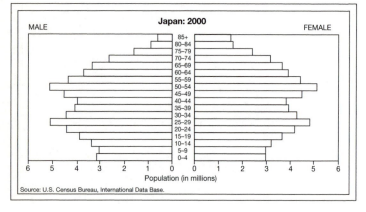

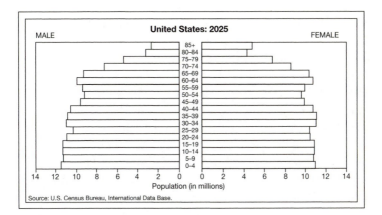

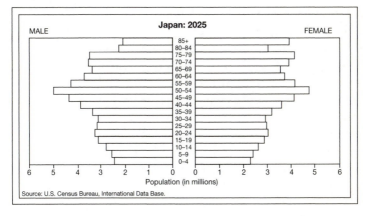

Figure 3.2 Population pyramids: selected countries 2000 and 2025.
Source: US Census Bureau, International Data Base, generated by author using Data Extraction System accessible at
<http://www/census.giv/ipc/www/idbpyr.html> (27 March 2002).

is shown by a leftward scale and female groups measured to the right. They are called population pyramids because in the past most took the shape of a pyramid, the youngest ages being the largest, tapering systematically to the smallest groups at the top. This shape is seen in the first diagram that illustrates the age profile of India in the year 2000. The pyramids in Figure 3.2 are for selected countries in 2000 and 2025 and illustrate how age profiles are now changing dramatically. High rates of fertility lead to many babies being born and a relatively large base to the pyramid; high death rates mean that the pyramid tapers rapidly to a point. As the rapid expansion of the world population slows down and life expectancy increases, the profile changes. The profile of a modern stable population, one which remains about the same size over an extended period of time yet has a relatively long life expectancy, would be closer to a column than a pyramid. The population of China is obviously much greater than that of the UK, so the scales are controlled to emphasise the comparative age profiles rather than the absolute size of the populations illustrated. India shows the classic pyramid shape but becomes more of a column by 2025. China shows the effects of the one-child policy which has produced wide differences in the size of generations. The contrast between the UK and the USA shows the effects of different demographic history; in particular the meaning of the 'baby-boom' post-war generation is illustrated. Japan currently has about the longest life expectancy of any nation. The 2025 pyramid in this case becomes inverted as subsequent cohorts with very low fertility lead to a decline in the size of the population.[10]

IS THERE A GLOBAL DEMOGRAPHIC CRISIS?

Population is a social phenomenon. The size of populations and how they change are the result of social processes. Population trends may have predictable features given in biological reproductive capacity and timed by the constraints of the human reproductive life span. However, population change is the result of changes in three demographic variables. These are the birth rate, the death rate and the balance of migration. Rises in the average age of a population may be because the younger age groups are getting smaller – perhaps fewer babies are born or because they do not survive infancy. Or, such rises could be the result of factors by which the older age group becomes larger than before. Of course, once born, a generation cannot increase in size, except by immigration. In practice historically most population ageing stems from a combination of fewer babies per mother and the fact that more of the age group survive from childhood into old age. Most developed countries in the world now have fertility rates below replacement level – fewer babies than is necessary to sustain the current size of the population. Places with such low fertility rates have ageing populations because the subsequent generations are smaller than the preceding ones. In Britain over the next thirty years the size of the age categories will shift significantly towards the elderly. The principal factor behind this change is a decline in the fertility rate. Between 1971 and 1991 the under-15s age group decreased in size by about 2.6 million people. In the same period the number of people aged over 65 increased by only 1.5 million. As a consequence the average age of the population rose almost twice as much because there were fewer young people than it did because there were more elderly people.[11] The consequence of relatively high fertility in the early 1950s and the baby boom of the 1960s followed by a long, sustained period of low fertility is a bulge generation that will reach retirement age from the year 2010 onwards.

In the twentieth century, one of the major determinants of the age of a population has been the infant mortality rate – this is number of deaths of those aged under 1 year per 1000 live births. Historically high rates of deaths soon after birth has meant that the size of older age groups has been restricted by the small proportions of people who survived infancy. Even in the UK today the most common age of death is still the first year of life. The decline in infant mortality rates has been dramatic in the twentieth century in Britain and Europe and across the world. Sixty or so years later, those who survived their first year of life and lived long enough, swell the ranks of the elderly. Keeping babies alive in the first half of the twentieth century had a large part to play in the ageing of populations in the second half. Thus the major causes of the increase in the average life span are the improvements in nutrition, hygiene and vaccination that mean people survive infancy.[12] In addition in recent years, the improving conditions of life and healthcare support for the elderly are to some extent helping to prolong the average life span. Life expectancy at age 60 increased by 2.4 years for men (from 15.3 years to 17.7 years) and 2.1 years for women (from 19.8 years to 21.9 years) between 1971 and 1991.[13] Thus there will be more, and a greater proportion of the oldest old, through this century. However, they are relatively few in absolute numbers. Mullan suggests that the recent falls in old-age mortality may be put into perspective by:

> contrasting figures for the change in male life expectancy at birth, and at age 65, over the 100 years 1861 to 1961. By the start of the 1960s on the basis of the average conditions of the time a new-born baby boy could expect to live 68 years. This is more than the 40.5 years of a century earlier. However, over the same period expectancy of the age of death for men who had reached their 65th birthday rose by only 1.4 years from 75.4 to 77 years.[14]

The decline in mortality of babies and young children in the early part of the twentieth century had a greater effect on life expectancy at birth than the contemporary decline in old age mortality. The speed at which death rates declined during infancy and childhood was generally faster than anything currently observed among older people. Most significantly reductions in death rates at a young age bring more average extra years of life than do similar reductions at older ages. A baby not killed by pneumonia could well survive to age 70, while saving a

70-year-old from breast cancer may perhaps increase that person's longevity by a further ten years.

Life expectancy is increasing at age 65 but it is not the major driving force for global population ageing. It is a very common fallacy to note the dramatic increase in the average length of life over the twentieth century and to put this down to survival in old age, and thus to make the further mistake of assuming that these increases in longevity will continue into the indefinite future. Wilmoth argues that although claims about fixed limits to human longevity have little scientific basis, a life expectancy at birth of around 85 years is within the range of values of the most reliable predictions for the mid-twenty-first century.[15] Wilder predictions about typical life spans reaching over a hundred years would require a much larger deviation from past trends. While researching my previous book on British politics and old age, a party campaign manager suggested during an interview that pension provision is now made more complicated by increasing life expectancy, and issues of an ageing population:

> I was at a seminar recently and one of the speakers said that he was convinced that average life expectancy would be 120 very shortly. And if that is the situation then clearly the whole thinking about how we deal with the pensions issue would have to go to a whole different level. That all the present thinking about funded pensions and how they work is clearly not going to keep people decently till they are 120.[16]

These gross misunderstandings of the demographic basis of an ageing population have consequences in terms of an inflated sense of expectation and inflated sense of crisis.

There are a variety of techniques for predicting future populations. They are all controversial with demographers, biologists and social scientists debating their various limitations. None have proved to be very accurate in the long term. Few population predictions have had a very long shelf life. Wilmoth states that a long history of data collection and modelling of over a century is the clearest evidence that mortality is declining and longevity increasing.[17] He argues that predictions based on short time spans are 'foolhardy' and reflect temporary baby booms and busts, but that the long-term trends have remained reasonably constant. He thus reaches the following predictions of future life expectancy that do not indicate dramatic changes in longevity in the immediate future.

> Recent forecasts by the U.S. Social Security Administration put life expectancy in 2050 at 77.5 years for men and 82.9 years for women, compared to 72.6 and 79.0 years in 1995 (2). These Social Security Administration forecasts are not true extrapolations, however, because they assume a slowdown in age-specific rates of mortality decline in the future. An independent study, based on a purely extrapolative technique, yielded more optimistic results (U.S. life expectancies at birth in 2050 of 84.3 years for both sexes combined) (3). Projections for Japan are only slightly higher (life expectancy at birth in 2050 of 81.3 years for men and 88.7 years for women, compared to 76.4 and 82.9 years in 1995) (4).[18]

There are disputes among biologists and demographers as to the extent to which the maximum natural life span has been reached. Some argue that there are inbuilt biological constraints on human longevity,[19] others that there appears to be no sign of an approaching finite limit to increases in longevity.[20] Wilmoth cautions against a too optimistic view that life span will increase rapidly in the near future, arguing that from a historical perspective this change is recent and should be extrapolated into the future with caution.

Past increases in longevity have derived from external threats to health, such as infectious diseases that shortened the lives of children. Olshansky states that 'another quantum leap in life expectancy at birth' of 20 to 30 years or more would have to be gained at the oldest ages, because mortality for people from infancy to age 30 is now extremely low.[21] The major causes of death are now inherent in the limitations of the body, arising from degenerative diseases and chronic illnesses – the diseases of ageing. Although Olshansky allows that impressive gains at the oldest ages are 'theoretically possible', he suggests that 'nothing currently on the scientific horizon would result in the modification of the biological aging process necessary to expand human aging so dramatically'. Population ageing advances more and more slowly at higher ages. The striking rise in the number of centenarians will have little effect on average life expectancy, Olshansky points out, 'because most of those now reaching their 100th birthdays are the kind of hearty individuals who previously died in their late 90s'. He calculated that given current trends, average life expectancy at birth would rise to age 85 in the USA by the year 2189. (The more long-lived Japanese would reach 85 in 2033, the French in 2035.) One of Olshansky's contributions to the debate on longevity has been to emphasise that average life expectancy in the USA would not reach 100 years 'until well after everyone alive today has already died'.[22]

Olshansky and Carnes' core argument in *The Quest for Immortality* is that science has manufactured extra life time already.[23] That although the natural life span is not a fixed entity because genetic variations between people give different individuals various chances of surviving various hazards, science now ensures we all have a good chance of surviving previous mortal hazards. Thus seen in evolutionary terms our bodies suffer from continued use beyond our planned operating lifetime. Science in various breakthroughs has enabled people to survive trauma which would have killed them in the past, to obtain a few more years of life, perhaps through dialysis or heart surgery. Olshansky and Carnes are clear that the first longevity revolution comes primarily from public health measures and control of infectious disease. They suggest that to see similar gains in longevity made in the twenty-first century there must be science-based modification of the genetic potential of the human species. This may be theoretically possible but such modification has not been achieved and does not represent a realistic possibility for many people beyond an experimental few for several centuries into the future.[24]

More immediate and dramatic changes to the age profile of a population can be made by social engineering rather than genetic engineering. Migration can alter the age of a population. The United Nations Population Division has conducted a study on the question of whether replacement migration could reverse trends towards population decline and population ageing.[25] Replacement migration was defined as the level of international migration that would be needed to offset declines in the size of a population, declines in the population of working age, as well as to offset the overall ageing of a population. The study came to the conclusion that if retirement ages remain essentially where they are today, increasing the size of the working-age population through international migration is the only option in the short to medium term to sustain a balance between working-age populations and those who are over retirement age. The study looked at countries where current fertility ranges from 1.2 to 2.0 children per woman. For France, the UK, the USA and the European Union as a whole, the numbers of migrants needed to offset population decline are less than or comparable to recent past experience. This is also the case for Germany and the Russian Federation, whose migration flows in the 1990s were relatively large due to reunification and dissolution, respectively. However, for some countries which have experienced particularly rapid and deep drops in fertility, specifically Italy, Japan and the Republic of Korea, a level of immigration much higher than experienced in the recent past would be needed to offset population decline.

CONCLUSION: OLDER PEOPLE IN AN UNEQUAL WORLD

The answers to the question about the impact of globalisation on old age identify the ways in which particular groups of older people feel the impact disproportionately. In particular older people in the rural Third World are most at risk. 'Too many old people' are seen by many as the cause of a crisis; instead they hould be thought of as a solution. Development which is socially nd environmentally sustainable requires zero or limited population growth. However, to curb world population growth equires a decline in human fertility until it reaches a sustainable or 'zero growth' level. Thus such a sustainable population would be an old population by historical standards. Concerns about environmental stability posed by population growth in the developing world have receded with worldwide reductions in fertility rates. The results of this global decline in fertility are seen in ageing populations across the world. However, older people in the Third World are taking the risk consequences of reducing the global threat from over-population as their smaller families may be less reliable sources of support in old age and other institutional support may not be available.

There has been much debate about the social significance of the ageing of populations. Many commentators identify it as a 'problem'. In particular, debates about appropriate government responses to ageing populations centre around public expenditure and welfare.

> In recent decades, the populations of developed countries have grown considerably older, because of increasing survival to older ages as well as smaller numbers of births. Consequently, both legislators and the general public have begun to consider society's role in the support of this ever-expanding elderly population. In this new demographic context, questions about the future of human longevity have acquired a special significance for public policy and fiscal planning.[26]

Looking at population ageing as a financial problem leads to policy agendas which treat older people as a burden and which deal largely with savings and pensions. Although ageing populations are an international phenomenon these agendas tend to be national in orientation, advisers making recommendations about what national governments should do in financial terms about the supposed consequences of population change. Dominant in the economic literature on old age has been the so-called 'intergenerational equity' debate. This involves issues about citizenship and community on the one hand, and pensions, health and social welfare of older people on the other. These issues have profound but poorly understood consequences for global society and will be discussed in Chapter 4. However, the import of this chapter is that globalisation as a social trend, while generating greater economic, social and environmental integration of all the people in the world has specific and in some cases adverse effects on ways people can live their old age.

4

OLD AGE, EQUITY AND INTERGENERATIONAL CONFLICT?

Working-Class Heroes: Peterlee was a New Town in Co. Durham, built to provide better housing for former miners. When I worked there in the 1970s I organised a voluntary visiting scheme for older people. I visited Tom regularly in his one-bedroomed old people's bungalow. He always sat in the same chair, wheezing with miner's lung – a big man but one who didn't move around much these days. He told many good stories. I asked him one day if he had known Peter Lee, the miners' leader after whom the town was named. I didn't get the reply I expected. 'Yes', he had met 'the bugger'. He was the magistrate that turned down Tom's request for compassionate leave when he came home from the army during the First World War to find his mother unwell.

THE DEMOGRAPHIC CRISIS AND NATIONAL PENSION SCHEMES

How best to secure a decent old age and well-funded retirement in the modern world? Does demographic change make this impossible for everyone? What role should the state or the private market play to ensure a good old age? What are the contending interests in the welfare provision for older people and what part do old people play? Can we expect generations to be in conflict? This chapter seeks to advance our understanding of old age by placing its dilemmas in the context of international pension fund capitalism. Population ageing has macro-economic implications for society as a whole alongside implications for individuals. It affects both public and private sector activities and goes beyond the formal economy to informal and domestic economic activity, and is fundamental to the way in which societies run and sustain themselves across generations.

Throughout the 1990s there has been considerable debate about the so-called issue of 'generational equity'. This debate appears at first sight to be about how governments will be able to sustain pension schemes in the face of ageing populations. It is suggested that individual savings rather than state-run pension schemes are the only way to survive the 'burden' of ageing populations. Further it is suggested that it is unfair to future generations to expect them to pay for the pensions of the large and affluent baby-boom generation. However, these arguments turn out not to be demographic or even strictly economic but rather ideological. They have embedded in them fundamental debates about the nature of society, what holds society together and what constitutes the values and lifestyle of the 'good' society. The outcome of current debates and political conflicts over securing well-funded retirement turns out to be unexpectedly critical for the future of global capitalism.

Pensions can be provided by many types of institution for many types of people; states for their citizens, corporations for their employees, commercial enterprises for their customers. These institutions, be they private or public, voluntary or compulsory, for profit or not for profit, may choose either Pay As You Go (PAYG) or funded schemes. The major actors who identify the problem of population ageing for the provision of financial security in old age (for example the World Bank) advocate some movement towards pensions schemes based on privately owned and managed investment funds. The crisis is presented as a particularly urgent problem for those countries with state-sponsored PAYG pensions schemes. Thus the first step in an examination of ways to secure financial security in old age is to contrast the social and economic effects of different approaches to providing pensions. Countries, or other institutions such as firms, which establish pension schemes have a number of choices. Each has benefits and drawbacks. If a PAYG system is established, each generation of citizens or employees has its pensions paid by the subsequent generation's contributions. The first generation thus gets its pension 'free' without having to contribute. Similarly if the system is suddenly stopped, the last generation paying loses its contributions but gets nothing back in the form of a pension. However, such PAYG systems are quickly established, and as prosperity grows it is possible for the older generation to benefit from the increasing wealth of the economy as a whole. For similar reasons they deal reasonably well with inflation, since both contributions and pensions can be changed in line with the changing value of money. If there is continuity and equal size of the generations then there is no problem of equity with PAYG schemes. However, if one generation is larger than the one before and/or the one after there are potential problems. A large working generation will find it relatively easy to pay good pensions for a smaller preceding one, but individuals within it will not unreasonably expect a similar standard of pension. If the subsequent generation is smaller than the retiring one, then they will, as individuals, have to pay a higher proportion of their income as contributions to sustain the pensions of the larger retired generation.

A funded pension scheme takes a generation to establish. Pensions are then paid from the savings made by contributing citizens, employees or subscribers during their working life, and from investment returns on the accumulated funds. In practice they are essentially a mechanism for smoothing income for individuals across a lifetime. Issues of generational equity do not seem to arise so readily with funded schemes. However, such systems do not deal well with situations of general and continuing rises in prosperity, as they leave the pensioner generation with a standard of living related to previous lower levels of income and thus relatively poorer compared to younger working generations. Historically in some countries inflation has wiped out the value of money and funded pensions schemes can be vulnerable to such crises. Funded schemes also, as is discussed below, are liable to potential problems in the face of recession and economic decline.

The dilemmas of intergenerational equity are thus a combination of two problems: first, the size and prosperity of successive generations, and second, the reliability and long-term security of the institutions which deliver the pension. The size of the 'baby-boom' generation is larger than the generations which precede and succeed it.[1] Thus it is argued that the PAYG entitlements of this group should be cut back to minimise the penalty on the post-baby-boom generation. In practice many governments have taken such action. To make up the shortfall the current generation in work is directed and offered financial incentives to move into funded pension schemes. There is a resulting generation inequity in so far as the working generation is being asked both to pay the pensions of the current retired generation and to save for its own retirement. This simplistic demographic model differs from the realities of intergenerational relationships in many significant ways and pays no account to the institutional mechanisms which organise and legitimise economic transfers between people.

The perceived crisis in the provision of pensions and decent old age in the face of demographic change is constructed in particular ways by analysts and commentators. For example, McMorrow and Roeger locate the problem as demographic in origin and a potential clash of interests between generations.[2] They ask: 'How much should the present generation transfer in terms of physical and human capital in order to ensure that the retirement of the "baby boom" generation doesn't pose insurmountable problems?'[3] They see the issue as essentially an economic one tied to state administration of the economy, stating that 'there is no "quick fix" available to reduce the inevitable economic burden of ageing'. They argue that an increase in productivity or savings is the only means available for economies to offset the pressures of ageing on future working-age populations. They suggest governments will need to reduce debt, cut pension and health provision, change labour laws to get more people into work (including raising the retirement age), together with other economic policies to raise economic growth rates. They see the solutions as difficult and long term and as a burden on future generations, and question whether the 'changes in the distribution of societies [*sic*] resources, between the employed and dependent populations, will be capable of being resolved without major crises and inter-generational conflicts'.[4] In common with many others they see funded pension schemes as the solution and anticipate 'that, over the next 50 years, all countries will move at least partially away from the . . . PAYG system'.[5] These positions represent something of an orthodoxy within the world of government and finance. Global financial regulatory institutions such as the World Bank have sought to set international models for pensions regimes along these lines.[6] The economic argument is that retirement savings stimulate investment and economic growth and thus society can better afford pensions payments. It is presented to individual citizens that the only way to secure one's own prosperity in old age given the instability of state PAYG schemes is to save through a private pension fund.

THE ISSUE IS NOT DEMOGRAPHIC – THE MANUFACTURE OF A CRISIS

However, the social issues of securing an income in old age are not of their essential nature demographic. It is the implicit view of old age, left embedded in the economic and financial analyses, that enables a crisis to be depicted. Old age, as we have seen, is socially constructed. Mere chronological age has little to do with being useful and productive. Even if we use the highly distorting view of 'productive activity' as simply 'paid employment', as Jackson points out, it is the institutionalised age restrictions imposed by formal retirement policies, employment practices and education arrangements that have constructed ageing as a problem. An old age that involves more choice over work and retirement would contribute positively not only by introducing greater flexibility to the economy but also increased possibilities of social contributions by older people. By de-institutionalising age it should be possible to focus on genuine social issues such as poverty or disability and tackle these rather than adding to the negative stereotypes of old age as a burden.[7]

Kirk Mann, among many others, argues for both the right to retire and a flexible age of retirement. International trends for early withdrawal from the labour market seem to be widespread in the developed world.[8] Early retirement may be a blessing or a curse. For many, early retirement is a form of disguised unemployment. Indeed there are strong parallels to retirement and unemployment. In times of high unemployment retirement is used explicitly as a tool with which to manage the employment market. Unemployment is a persistent feature of capitalist economies and there are times when the unemployed population outnumbers the retired population. Why, asks Jackson should we single out population ageing as causing a special crisis when economic dependency among the unemployed and other sections of the population such as children, students and mothers is viewed as part of the normal functioning of the economy?[9] In the contemporary world, economic growth is as likely to be labour displacing as it is to be employment creating. Old age is not a special case, it is not the only or even the predominant cause of people becoming dependent financially on others. The balance between those working and those on benefits has strong social and institutional aspects and is not the same as the balance between productive and unproductive members of society. As Jackson says, 'Both unemployment and retirement are socially created, and they are not reducible to the behaviour or physical characteristics of unemployed and retired individuals'.[10]

The ageing of populations is not new. It has been the characteristic of the British population for most of the twentieth century, which saw the establishment and maturation of the British pension system. Mullan points out that 'British society had coped with a tripling in the proportion of over-64s between 1911 and 1991' and that 'in comparison a further 50 per cent rise over the next 50 years does not seem that onerous'.[11] Although crises of increased dependency ratios have been regularly predicted during this period they have never materialised. The prime reason for this is that growth in economic efficiency has been more than enough to ensure that the productivity of those in work has increased and produced the resources to fund ever-increasing standards of living in retirement.

Historically modern societies double their wealth about every 25 years. This pace of expansion projected into the next half-century dwarfs the extra cost for society from more elderly dependants.[12]

The proposed solution for the 'demographic time bomb' crisis, that of funded pension schemes, leaves the original problem of the demographic balance between generations unaltered. There will still be the same ratio of workers to pensioners (as defined by simplistic 'dependency ratio' measures). If the projected labour shortage materialises, wage inflation will push down the relative value of pension assets compared to the price of labour. Demand from affluent pensioners for the labour of diminishing numbers of workers will push up their price. In other words it will become relatively more expensive to employ a nurse, a doctor or a hang-glider instructor than previously. It remains highly uncertain whether funded pension schemes will create a larger volume of future goods and services for retired people or merely re-allocate who gets them. What they clearly cannot do is change the demography. To make the case that privately managed pension schemes offer a better long-term option for older people in general rather than a limited number of affluent individuals, it has to be shown that greater gains to societal productivity can be made through the route of private pension fund investment than alternatives. This case is far from made.[13]

The view of population ageing as a demographic time bomb has been constructed by those with a particular agenda and a specific way of seeing the world. The function of such arguments is to create a sense of inevitability and scientific certainty that public pension provision will fail. In so far as this strategy succeeds it creates a self-fulfilling prophesy. If people believe the 'experts' who say publicly sponsored PAYG systems cannot be sustained, they are more likely to act in ways that mean they are unsustainable in practice. Certainly in Britain and elsewhere in Europe the state pension is an extremely popular institution. To have it removed or curtailed creates massive opposition. Only by demoralising the population with the belief that it is demographically unsustainable has room for the private financiers been created and a mass pensions market formed.

GLOBALISATION AND THE NATION STATE, IMPLICATIONS FOR WELFARE

The idea of the welfare state

To what extent can and should nation states provide the means for securing a good old age? Should people be able to claim an old age pension merely because they are citizens? Alternatively does the market, given that 'shares can go up or down in value', offer a secure way to finance retirement? In practice low income groups in most countries are never going to be able to fund their own retirement. There needs to be some element of redistribution if all older people are to receive an adequate income. Even the World Bank in setting out its policy for pensions recognises the need for 'mandatory tax-financed public [pensions] designed to alleviate poverty'.[14] The original state pension systems founded in Germany in the 1880s were constructed to bolster the established political order and counter the political appeal of socialist programmes to the poor.[15] The welfare state in Britain was founded and developed in the period immediately following the Second World War.

The welfare state was conceived in the darkest moments of the Great Depression, and forged as an institution in the aftermath of the Second World War. At its peak, its many functions and responsibilities literally institutionalized the social relations of Western societies. For many, the state was both *the proper provider* of public infrastructure, and, given the vagaries of the market, the only institution *capable of providing* a comprehensive system of public goods. . . . Recent moves to radically reform (UK) and even dismantle (US) welfare programmes suggest, in fact, that the post-war consensus that legitimized state inter-vention in market capitalism is in tatters.[16]

Pensions in Britain became part of the idea of a welfare state that cared for people 'from the cradle to the grave'. The idea was (and still is) extremely popular with British people. Social theorists elaborated the idea of a 'social citizenship' which also provided a justification of post-war governments that pursued social democratic policies. Marshall, for example, suggested that in Britain there had been a historical progression of free-dom, moving from civil to political to social rights between the eighteenth and twentieth centuries.[17] That post-war Britain represented the triumph of social development was taken as read.[18] The inequalities created through the industrial revolu-tion and the market were to be contained by the state in order to establish social harmony. Citizens were to have a stake in society; one which removed the desire to change radically the institutional order or to challenge the centrality of the market.[19] What has changed to undermine the welfare state is not social citizenship *per se*, but rather the state and its ineffectiveness in delivering social rights and sustaining itself and those rights in the face of a changing world.

Changes in the welfare state: the British case

The consequence of the New Right approach to the apparent demography crisis has been to undermine and fundamentally change the nature of the welfare state in the United Kingdom. The degree to which the British provision for income maintenance in old age has been undermined over the twenty years from 1980 to 2000 is not always understood in the UK. An American commentator, Stevenson, suggests that 'alone among the biggest industrialized nations, Britain has taken aggressive steps over the last two decades to shift responsibility for retirement income from government to individuals'.[20] Many have linked these changes to the ideologies of the new right.[21] Stevenson suggests that the consequence is that 'the financial burden of providing pensions to an ageing population will decrease in Britain in relation to the size of the economy'.[22] What he means of course is that what has changed is the *government's* future liabilities; the problem for society and for individuals of securing a decent old age in the future remains.

In Britain, successive Labour and Conservative governments offered additional and alternative schemes over and above the basic National Insurance provision which was left to form a smaller and smaller part of post-retirement income. People were encouraged to 'opt out' of the state system's earnings-based component and instead pay part of their National Insurance contribution into a company-sponsored retirement plan. Employer-based schemes linked to final salaries were the source of much new-found pensioner prosperity in the late 1990s. The Conservative administrations of the 1990s offered major financial incentives in terms of tax relief to those taking out private pension schemes. In addition, the prolonged stock market boom of the 1990s was a lure for people to put their savings into private pension plans. Such were the stock market gains that it seemed self-evident that this was a better option than state-provided pensions. Unfortunately many of those who purchased such pensions were poorly advised and a mis-selling scandal ensued. There was little organised resistance to the changes and the devaluation of the state pension. This fitted very nicely with the analysis which said that state pensions were unsustainable and that the solution was for workers to take responsibility for themselves, thus reducing the gap between the benefits due to future generations and the tax yield on a shrinking workforce.[23]

The post-1997 Labour government continued previous financial policies and in particular there was a strong desire to limit and contain the long-term financial obligations of the state, and to facilitate the participation of private capital and to encourage private provision to substitute for public wherever possible. However, the Chancellor of the Exchequer, Gordon Brown, did deem the pension funds sufficiently affluent to introduce a major new tax measure which diverted part of their previous income stream into the Treasury. The Blairite 'Third Way' seems to accept that there are severe limits on what the welfare state can provide in future (whether this is due to demography or an unwillingness to raise taxation is unclear). The consequence is to seek to limit welfare to a minority, as a safety net for a small group at the bottom of society, and to encourage self/private provision for the majority. The thrust of pension reform seems unclear, but the prime initiative, 'the stakeholder' pension, is to extend individual saving for old age further down the social scale. However, the stakeholder scheme has met with limited success and an initial unwillingness of companies to sell the product, and an unwillingness of small business to involve itself in employees' pensions. The value of the basic state pension entitlement continues to be eroded, while the central plank of income maintenance policies for older people has become 'the guaranteed minimum income' which is in fact a complex means-tested safety net for those with inadequate private means.

There is some irony in the fact that the UK has among the lowest current and projected dependency ratios in the developed world, and a state insurance scheme in surplus, but persists in the view that the state should try to minimise its role in the provision of pensions.[24] Despite much of the previous rhetoric about 'demographic time bombs', most informed commentators believe that the UK government does not have a significant financing problem in its public pension system. The range of measures taken, in particular the removal of automatic upgrading of pensions in line with earnings and equalisation of age of retirement for men and women at the higher age of 65, will curtail entitlements such that existing contribution rates will more than cover for demographic change. Britain's demographic position and the position of its public pension provision means that it does not share some of the accumulated public liabilities built up by other countries within the European Union. By 2030, when most of the post-war generation will have retired, the British government's pension costs are projected to be 6.2 per cent of Gross Domestic Product (GDP), compared with 6.8 per cent in the USA, 14.2 per cent in Germany and 17.2 per cent in France.[25]

GLOBALISATION AND THE GROWTH OF PENSIONS AS A FORCE IN WORLD FINANCIAL MARKETS

The contemporary crisis in the welfare state with which the current governments of the world are wrestling lies in the political failure of the nation state in the face of global capital. One of the impacts of globalisation has been to force states to withdraw from welfare, including provision for old age.[26] There is a loss of power by nation states vis-à-vis other institutions in their ability to command resources and exert control. Isin and Wood argue that there is considerable anxiety about the decline of the sovereignty of nation states in formulating and implementing public policy independent of transnational corporations and organisations.[27] They see that the capacity of modern nation states to regulate economic and social matters has been significantly curtailed.[28] The globalisation of financial markets has had a general impact on national economic policies and in particular the way states finance their own activities. It has forced states to minimise their own role in mediating financial redistributions and remove unfunded future financial liabilities such as pensions that are seen to influence their creditworthiness. Fiscal rectitude (and thus keeping themselves solvent and the financial markets stable) means that governments are required to keep their borrowing low. In particular the need to attract investment from the global capital market is seen by governments as preventing them from departing too far from internationally competitive standards of taxation and redistribution. In a market-orientated globalised world, the nation state has sought ways actively to displace inherited responsibilities to citizens and pass them to individuals and to the market. Hirst and others see global capitalism as the excuse for the national political elite to pursue their real agenda rather than international capital acting as a genuine constraint.[29] Such arguments suggest that national government could act to socially direct capital if it had the motivation to do so. In my view this is an outdated understanding of the power of the nation state which sees it potentially as the embodiment of a national collective will through which politics is the governor of the economy. Unfortunately only global politics – global social solidarity – can curtail the power of international financial capital.

Crisis in the provision of public pensions has to be seen in the context of the optimism behind the enormous expansion of privately controlled pension funds. Since the early 1980s, British and American private pension assets have 'attained stupendous size and importance', eclipsing all other forms of private savings and transforming the nature and structure of global financial markets. Minns quotes the figure of $12,000 billion for worldwide pension assets – 'more than the combined value of all the companies quoted on the world's three largest stock markets'.[30] Funded pensions in America grew from only $20 billion in assets in 1950 to over $7 trillion in 2000 – 70 per cent of the US GDP. In the last twenty years of the twentieth century, UK individual pension and retirement assets increased about twelvefold to around $1.5 trillion. Managing these assets is, not surprisingly, staggeringly lucrative. The UK market for investment consulting is estimated to be worth around £80 million a year, for actuarial services of approximately £250 million and an estimated £4.9 billion for institutional fund management.[31]

Australia and Canada have also followed this pattern with high rates of asset growth. The growth of pension assets has profoundly changed the financial structure of all these countries. The significance of pension fund capitalism in different countries is illustrated by Table 4.1 constructed with OECD data. For each country the value of the assets of pension funds and of all institutional investors (those whose business is looking after and investing money such as insurance companies and building societies) is compared to a measure of the amount of wealth the country produces (GDP). Thus the relative importance of pension funds and other forms of institutional investment to particular economies can be identified.

Table 4.1 Financial assets of institutional investors (% of GDP)

	Pension funds		Total institutional investment	
	1998	1990	1998	1990
Sweden	2.7	1.7	139.0	85.7
Italy	3.2	3.5	80.3	13.4
Germany	3.3	3.1	70.2	36.5
Korea	4.0	3.1	108.6	48.0
Belgium[a]	4.8	2.0	74.5	44.4
Norway	7.2	4.4	47.6	36.0
Japan[b]	18.9	..	38.7	81.7
Denmark	21.5	14.6	87.3	55.6
Canada	47.7	28.8	111.9	58.1
Australia	55.4	17.0	115.1	49.3
United Kingdom	83.7	55.0	214.2	114.5
Netherlands	85.6	81.0	155.8	133.4
United States of America	86.4	44.9	218.8	119.4

Source: OECD 2000, accessible at
<http://www.sourceoecd.org/data/cm/00000819/OECD_in_figures_2000.pdf>
Notes:
[a] For Belgium the later figures are from 1997 data.
[b] For Japan in 1990 the pension fund percentage of GDP was not available while the 1998 total figure of institutional investors excludes insurance companies.

In France, Germany and other major European economies, state-run PAYG schemes are the central pillar of income in retirement. Despite high standards of living and high employment rates, the different structure of retirement finance means they have not experienced the very high rates of growth of pension assets. Some, including major multinational institutional players such as the EU, the IMF and the OECD, argue that private funded pensions are essential and that the long-term prosperity of European nations is threatened by 'inefficient and institutionally cumbersome finance sectors'.[32] That is, not only do they see demographic challenges to the European systems, they also see the British and American systems as creating greater economic dynamism and an economic competitive challenge. Similar arguments are made for East Asia and Japan where there is also an absence of private pension funds. In that region enterprises tend to carry unsecured liabilities for future pensions to their employees when they retire. Such policies are in line with the paternalistic employment patterns found in Japan, where investment is dominated by a large banking sector; bank assets are larger than those of stock and bond markets combined. By contrast in the USA, stock and bond markets are four times larger than bank assets because of the pension structure.[33] Japan has the oldest average age of all industrial nations, and both the demography and the financial structure of pensions in that country have been advanced as reasons for the Asian economic crisis at the end of the 1990s.

The social changes behind pension fund capitalism

This enormous growth of private pension assets reflects:

- the demography of the 'baby boom';
- the rapid post-1950 expansion of employment;
- increased participation in employer-based private pension schemes;
- changing legal and institutional basis for pension savings and financial markets in general.

In other words this tidal wave of international capital reflects a generation feature of society: the demography of the baby-boom generation, its employment opportunities and opportunities for saving, together with legal and administrative changes which enhanced its welfare interests. Population growth in the post-Second World War era created expanded markets, enlarged the labour force and increased the opportunities for economic growth.

From the free marketeers' perspective the spread of private funded pensions to dominate the global economy, and the finance industry in particular, is based on four global trends.

1. *The demand for pensions*. Global ageing and steadily increasing life expectancy is an opportunity for the finance industry, driving demand for its pensions products. From the same perspective the competition from other sectors is in trouble because global ageing is straining PAYG public pension systems and corporate pension systems.
2. *The demand for investment capital*. Increasing international investment which has expanded dramatically in recent years is driven on the one hand by investment managers seeking to diversify risk by investing in a range of countries and on the other hand industries all over the world looking to global capital markets for finance. In 1990, US external investment by pension funds was less than $350 billion but is rapidly approaching $2 trillion in 2002.
3. *New technological and institutional opportunities*. The increasingly complex investment strategies adopted by those controlling capital can be related to changing information technology and new financial instruments. Changes in financial services technology, and the rapid evolution of new types of financing such as 'derivatives', 'futures', 'hedge funds' and so on channel funds to new markets. These new methods of trading in money from one perspective may be thought to aid speculation and financial instability. From another point of view they intro-duce a new and beneficial fluidity to capital markets. They

enable good investment opportunities to find the capital to back them.

4. *Opportunities for growth.* The creation of funded pensions that are financed by investment returns, rather than by redistributions mediated by government, increases the stock of capital and, it is argued, increases the rate of saving in the economy. The free market sees a 'virtuous circle' of increased investment, stock market growth and increased capital gains such as was powering the American economy in 1990s.[34]

PROBLEMS WITH THE ECONOMIC ARGUMENTS FOR PENSION FUND CAPITALISM

Many identify the triumph of American capitalism with the success of the pension fund industry. It has brought capitalism and its benefits to the masses. They therefore argue that this success can be exported and form part of a globalisation of capital. However, there are considerable problems associated with these developments. The collective rationality of economic individualism, namely individuals being responsible for their own financial provision in old age, is problematic. The overall consequences of individuals looking after their own interests may have unintended social consequences. These may be understood as a series of contradictions; that is, ways in which the social change undermines itself: the more it succeeds and expands the greater the social difficulties that arise.

- There is a contradiction between savings as a source of investment and savings as deferred consumption. Put another way, stock-market values, and families, go through cycles. Sometimes stock markets boom, sometimes they slump, and sometimes families need to cash in their savings, sometimes they can save. Unfortunately there is no mechanism by which these are synchronised. No-risk investments yield poor returns.
- Further, there is a contradiction between social cohesion and

long-term financial security for older people on the one hand and the increasingly global and 'efficient' financial markets through which their pension funds are invested on the other. Markets both need and undermine social solidarity.

• Finally, there is a contradiction between the need to save and people's ability to see their savings work in their own interests rather than against them. It may be in the interests of their pension fund that the factory in which they work closes.

I will deal with each of these in turn.

Generational cycles of investment and disinvestment

Free market accounts of the benefits of private funded pension schemes are partial. They appear to be authoritative because they come from people who wield enormous financial power. However, they do not dwell on the implications of stock-market failure. Most pension funds have experienced loss of value in their stock-market-based assets in the two years to 2001, and in 2002 there is a growing sense of crisis in private provision as the stock market continues to decline. Further, there is very little analysis of the consequences of disinvestment when assets are realised for consumption. A private 'funded' pension scheme is in principle an income-smoothing device which enables individuals to save for old age. Such funds, like an individual, build up assets. Cash savings are used to buy stocks and shares, property, or government bonds – assets that will yield an income and can be sold as necessary. Acquisition of assets is fastest when there is most spare cash – which tends to be in middle age for individuals and in the early years of a pension fund. Savings and assets logically reach a peak at retirement age. A pension fund where pension payments start to outweigh contributions is said to be 'mature'. When cash is needed for daily living expenses, assets are sold to provide income. When a pension fund matures assets will be sold to provide cash for pensions. The savings of the person driven solely by self-interest will logically fall to zero at death.

For any individual the maximum rate of savings is likely to be greatest during peak earning years, probably while in their forties and fifties (and after child rearing). The rate of saving may well be expected to decline starting in the sixties, and the decline to accelerate into the seventies and eighties. This life-cycle model of saving/pension contributions suggests fastest accumulation up to approximately thirty years after inception of the pension fund. If we apply this model to the bulge cohort born between 1945 and 1950, it would suggest a start to pension contributions and saving in 1965 to 1970 with a peak in 1985 onwards to 2005–2010 when net selling assets can be anticipated (the timing obviously depends on factors such as early retirement patterns whereby retirement age continues to fall). The cohort would be expected to be selling assets at age 70 in the years 2015 to 2020.

> As the data from the Norwegian research shows . . . financial capital increases at regular intervals with increased age, up until the age of 67–79 years. Retired people do not spend their capital, and many continue to save during their retirement. Most retired people express the wish to help both their children and their grandchildren and to make sure that they will inherit.[35]

There are considerable problems with the 'life cycle' model of savings.[36] Most significantly this seems to stem in large part from a desire to support succeeding generations and pass an inheritance to children. Nevertheless, savings in the specific form of funded pension schemes, where the fund assets are held in the form of stocks, bonds and so on, will inevitably have to be sold to raise cash to pay for pensions. Further the size of the pool of savings will be related to the size of cohorts generating savings and those consuming pensions. The demographics of the 'bulge' generation will mean that in a mature system, unless the smaller subsequent generation saves even more than the current one to compensate, the net asset value of the funds must decline. The fund's assets must be realised to fund consumption during retirement and passed to pensioners as cash to be spent on subsistence, leisure, health and other forms of care in old age. However, as savings push up prices on the stock market, presumably disinvestment will bring them down, thereby reducing the value of savings and creating a negative spiral to mirror the upward spiral of the 1980 and 1990s. In practice, the stock-market downturn in the past two years has resulted in a push to restrict pensions benefits – the financial markets have led a number of large companies to cut final salary schemes in favour of less certain contribution calculated schemes.[37] In mid-2002 the pensions 'crisis' in the popular press is no longer a demographic one but rather one of stock-market failure.

Pension funds try to balance the risks of the stock market with less volatile investments. Of course, less risky investments mean lower yields and may not pay the best pensions. Pension funds have been required traditionally to keep a proportion of their funds in state bonds – gilt-edged securities – to ensure they keep risks low and do not lose the fund's assets in speculative gambles. This proportion varies from country to country and has a considerable impact on the fund's performance. In the UK in the 1990s, parallel to the boom in the stock market has been the reduction in the proportion of total liabilities formed by state borrowing. As the British government was so successful in reducing its debt, gilts came to be in short supply. In Britain rules about how much pension funds have to place in bonds have had to be changed because there were not enough of them to supply the need. Low government borrowing forces the increased volume of pension savings away from gilt-edged securities into other financial instruments. There has been a growing range of financial institutions and ways in which capital may be managed and invested. Some of these new financial tools have proved risky and provided uncertain returns. The paradox is that pension funds use low levels of national debt as an indicator of a healthy economy, while needing national debt to provide a bedrock of secure assets.

Social solidarity issues

Pension provision requires multi-generational social stability. It is clear that for financial security in old age there needs to be a readily understood, convincing ideology which makes people forgo current consumption to fund retirement either through savings or PAYG. Further, people need to believe that the institutional social relationships will endure and future obligations will be fulfilled – it is essential that these relationships are sustained over successive generations. The issue of social solidarity is therefore the most fundamental aspect of securing a good old age.

This issue should not be seen as one in which the 'market' is contrasted to 'social solidarity' as suggested by Clark.[38] Rather, all economic systems, whether they are institutionalised around markets, states, families, communities or castes, are underpinned by different forms of social solidarity. The state and the market, as the dominant forms of modern pension provision, both require a basic underpinning of social cohesion. Capitalist motives of individual self-interest should not be taken for granted as the most efficient or secure way to achieve this cohesion. One of the major problems for private insurance companies and governments trying to promote private pensions as a progressive social policy is that people do not trust them. This mistrust is well placed; a contract with a private company underpinned by market pressure is no less likely to be dishonoured than a state guarantee backed by democratic pressure. Market mechanisms require a number of social prerequisites to work. One of the key founding figures of sociology, Emile Durkheim, identified the importance of precontractual social solidarity.[39] He argued that modern society had come to be based on mutual agreements, that is to say contracts, in contrast to traditional societies whose social solidarity depended on the power of tradition and coercion of those who deviated. However, later in his work he came to see the importance of moral underpinning to a contract, a collective feeling of right or wrong which formed the basis of trust and of law, and that enabled contracts to be made. So we can ask. What are the bases for the intergenerational contract which links successive generations and makes them willing to contribute financially to those in old age? These bases are essentially ideological; they legitimate access to resources.

Ideologies have practical and political consequences for the problem of persuading people to forgo current consumption for a promise of future income in old age. These ideologies are realised in specific social institutions which organise transfers of resources between people and justify them. For whom should a pension be a just reward for a meretricious life course? Should it be the mothers of the next generation? Soldiers who defended the motherland? Workers who built the new society? Prudent savers who deferred income invested wisely in anticipation of old age? or fellow citizens who should not fall below acceptable standards of welfare? These answers reflect a range of ideologies. Different societies have given different priority to a variety of social groups. There are ideologies that justify distributions to older people on the basis of different attributes. There is a continuing political conflict about the moral standing of different social groups and their rights of different kinds to access sources of income. In the contemporary world the following individualist ideologies are the most dominant:

- *Private property*. Ownership grants exclusive rights, which should have a market price. A good old age is secured through the accumulation of property.
- *Meritocracy*. Rewards should go to those who have worked hard and invested wisely. A good old age is secured through reward for merit, usually in terms of work and prudent use of assets and talents.

Capitalist society is organised around the principles of private property and wage labour. These form the dominant and frequently unquestioned source of rights to wealth and income in old age. Property is something which belongs to individuals and can be transferred between individuals by their freely given act of will. Moral evaluation is given in greatest measure to those who conserve and make the most of their property and talents. However, there are also powerful communal ideologies. Familial ideologies, which justify inheritance and family mutual support, are very strong. For example, there are family values that hold the virtue of mutual support by reason of blood ties. Spouses should support each other 'for richer, for poorer'. Nationalist ideologies and the rights of citizens also provide a channel by which claims are made to part of the total national output. The above debate about the proper role of the state in welfare was predicated on national and citizenship values – the nation should 'look after its own'.

The basis for trust in social and economic institutions varies from country to country and over time. The specific American experience of absence of war on their own territory, stable currency and the long-standing and powerful corporate sector gives them a view of the world which is different from those places which have experienced destruction of states, currencies wiped out by hyper-inflation, property and assets appropriated by invaders. It gives Americans confidence in their private pension funds, but makes German and French people tenacious in their belief in their state PAYG schemes.

The problem of social cohesion is reflected in the core social problem of growing global markets in finance, and pension funds in particular. The 'workers vs. pensioners' debate has a global dimension. The association of the demographically ageing affluent populations with the ex-colonial and imperial powers and the Anglo-American domination of the financial markets through access to capital from pension funds reinforces established global divisions. New developing economies with large expanding young populations may create an as-yet unexplored source of crisis if they seek to alter the balance of returns between capital and labour. Even within Europe there have been concerns expressed about the price local people pay in job losses and low wages to sustain the returns on investment by American and other overseas pension funds that have come to make up such a considerable proportion of international investments.[40] Age-based redistribution from young to old can take on an international dimension. Will workers and their political representatives tolerate their TV assembly plants in Kuala Lumpur or Canton being sold off or even closed to pay the pensions of older people in Milton Keynes or New Jersey? Will poor Third World workers willingly pay for the pensions of the affluent West into the future? Global redistributions of surplus value organised through pension fund capitalism may be characterised as exploitative or as important insurance mechanisms providing resources to support old age. They may be seen as being both simultaneously when Third World workers are the source of return on Western pension funds. What institutions can securely and fairly ensure this redistribution? Only large and global institutions can counter such political uncertainties and secure regular, legitimised international transfers. What ideologies can cement the required social solidarity to make such institutions effective? None of the ideologies discussed above provide a promising basis for guaranteeing that there is a universal perceived collective economic interest and moral responsibility for ensuring that global risks are not exacerbated. In terms of economic development, short-term disbenefits may be necessary to provide investment for the future. Who should we believe if we are promised jam tomorrow in return for a thinner slice of the cake today? Historical experience suggests that power and wealth tend to become concentrated by global markets. Collective responsibility for the risks that threaten the world is essential and should entail a collective responsibility towards all those who bear those risks. However, in reality we remain a very long way from any meaningful global citizenship.

As pension funds seek more and more investment opportunities worldwide, they require standard legal and contractual underpinning, standardised accounting techniques and rules about transparency so that they can assess risks within a standard frame of reference. Standardised financial procedures around the world increase transparency and trust in a financial system and thus facilitate the confidence to invest large amounts of capital through the financial markets. Successful pension fund capitalism and wealthy capital markets need a reliable regulatory framework, whereby the rules are transparent and strictly observed. Further, efficient markets need a constant flow of accurate, readily accessible information. Information flows have been facilitated by electronic mediums but still require standard and accurate accountancy and reporting of financial information. The failures of such accounting procedures in the USA involved the collapse of major corporations such as Enron and WorldCom and subsequent turmoil in financial markets. Although the markets require the state to provide the legal and regulatory framework in order to ensure predictable returns on investment, the financial elite regards it as essential that markets must be free of political manipulation. Hence the well-known features of globalisation for which such elites strive: standardisation of rules and regulations, the expansion of markets, constructed in a way which excludes democratic establishment of economic priorities.

The extent to which globalisation has undermined the possibility of the nation state being a welfare state and reliably providing for its citizens in old age is a key feature of the shift from public to private pension provision. However, the decline in the provision of welfare delegitimises the institution of the nation state. Ironically, given the role of the state in financial stability, the power of globalised capital and its particular manifestation in multinational pension funds is one of the factors undermining the perception of the nation state as a legitimate political institution. The inability of the state to provide for its citizens removes a significant part of its legitimacy. The declining relevance of the welfare state in providing health and security of people goes hand in hand with political alienation and thus political instability. The very activity of pension fund capitalism undermines the social basis which enables it to operate.

Despite, and indeed because of, its vulnerability to international finance, the state continues to play a crucial role in financial policy and stability. Not only is it responsible for the legal framework necessary for the finance industry, in practice, the state is the insurer of final resort, and unspoken underwriter for private pension liabilities. In a crisis, the state will act to preserve public confidence in the financial system and is thus very likely to bail out large failing pension funds. The finance industry collectively plays a part in sustaining confidence by limiting the consequences of market failure for pensioners through mechanisms to support failing financial institutions. Rather than have a complete collapse in confidence in the financial institutions, governments will always act. For example, Ashlag, discussing the potential inability of Israeli pension funds to meet their future liabilities, states that the 'political realities are such that no Israeli government is likely to let the Histadrut pension funds default on their retirement payments'.[41] The ability to sustain confidence in a financial industry is crucial where loss of trust in the value of money or the reliability of institutions to return savings placed with them would result in the nightmare of financial meltdown, a situation experienced in Argentina in December 2001.[42]

Conflicting interests

Economic power and political power go hand in hand. The economic power of pension funds interacts with both national and international political arenas. Coalitions of groups with common interests build up with growing pension funds. These coalitions may contain not only beneficiaries but also the financial class who live as managers and advisers, and political elites, particularly those looking for inward investment and who benefit from the expansion which investment brings. Leslie Sklair studied the development of an 'international capitalist class' as a set of people who actively promote globalisation.[43] Certainly to many influential elites, active support of pension fund capitalism came to look like the only way forward. Many national and regional elites saw active co-operation with global finance as a way to out-invest and out-compete rival economies. However, such coalitions may not prove solid when economic and investment cycles come to maturity. When pension funds need to dispose of assets, disinvestment will pull these coalitions apart. Faced with economic downturn, who will buy the assets? Will productive concerns be closed down – 'rationalised' – and a negative economic spiral instigated? In these circumstances, the coalitions that provide the political stability and legal underpinning, particularly to transnational investment, no longer have common interests with pension fund beneficiaries. The social solidarity underpinning the way the market is constructed falls apart. Nationalism, no repatriation of profits, repudiation of debts, programmes to nationalise industry without compensation, could all be reactions to economic downturn in the global economy as pension funds attempt to realise overseas assets. The common interest between the finance industry and fund beneficiaries may come apart, companies could try and restrict benefits, shareholders may try to protect their value against beneficiaries by directing people to the state as final guarantor of their pensions. The surviving, more cohesive, socially based PAYG pension systems may be able to sustain cohesion and continue to pay pensions in the downturn more successfully than those systems which are more dependent on financial markets. Multi-generational institutions capable of reliably supporting people in old age are unlikely to be sustained by fickle investor confidence in volatile financial markets.

OLD AGE AND THE POWER OF CAPITAL

This chapter has explored the power relationships that dominate the possibilities of living a financially secure old age. The power relationships operate on a global scale and have been characterised as 'pension fund capitalism'. However, there were a number of writers in the 1970s and 1980s who saw the growth of occupational pension funds as a form of workers' control and the growth of pensions as a 'new socialism'.[44] In the late 1990s Robin Blackburn resurrected this idea and argued that publicly controlled pension funds provide a route to 'socialise' capital, namely to make capitalism responsive to the real needs of the people. He advocates something resembling an ethically responsible national pension fund.

> In Singapore, the state-owned and managed Central Provident Fund furnishes a mechanism whereby each citizen is obliged to make provision for sickness and old age; their individual fund can also be drawn upon to finance acquisition of a house or the taking of an educational qualification. Such a system encourages individual involvement and responsibility, while allowing for flexibility. Whether this would promote egalitarianism depends on overall government policy which can always furnish correctives and controls. . . . The CPF invests 90% of its money in public bonds, though the government has used these bonds to make its own equity investments.[45]

Attractive as the prospect Blackburn offers is, the massive growth in pension fund power looks like a rather 'pure' form of capitalism. Pension funds do not act as the capitalism of the people. Neither does it follow that because they are the savings of a numerically significant proportion of the population, that they represent a utopia of collective ownership. There is a clear alienation of the producers of wealth from the results of their collective efforts which are then used to dominate and set the framework of the society in which they live out their old age. If the majority of workers could control world capital through their individual savings in pension funds, then capitalism would be run in the interests of all (as all are shareholders).[46] However, control of these accumulated capital funds does not lie with their nominal owners, namely the contributors. Pension fund capitalism appears to me to be a particularly pristine type of capitalism because of the enormous gulf between the apparent owners of 'capital' – the beneficiaries – and those who actually control the funds, who are in reality the fund managers. These fund managers do not have complete freedom of action; in fact they are tightly constrained by each other and operate according to codes of conduct which are precisely informed by the standard canons of neo-classical economics. Fund managers have been criticised for not being sufficiently entrepreneurial, in particular ignoring start-up or small enterprises and of following a herd instinct – watching each other so that their performance in comparative terms matches that of the other fund managers.[47] Their principal source of behavioural guidance is the theories and models of economics and finance as a professional discipline. They believe in the market and therefore believe the models and act as if they were real. Hence they become real.

In global terms the dominance of pension fund capitalism may be seen as a manifestation of the class relationship between North and South. Both the relationships between age groups, and generational opportunities for work and retirement have to be seen in the context of changing global demographics. If we talk in global terms rather than any looming shortage of workers, there are too few jobs available for those seeking work. Those workers may not be in the right place or possess the right skills but there are plenty of them and they are by and large young. Indeed the demand for work is so strong that draconian measures create a 'fortress Europe' to keep them out. The contrast within new-right discourses between arguments over immigration and population ageing is striking.[48]

An internationalist perspective is essential to provide a critical analysis of the limitations of nationalist, commercial and kinship ideologies in providing a secure old age in the modern world. It is needed to provide an insight into the bases of solidarity between generations required in the future and to expose the bias which defines an ageing population as a potential disaster rather than the human success it actually represents. It is evident that globalisation – the creation of a mutually interdependent world – results in global responsibilities. As co-residents on 'spaceship

Earth' we have responsibilities to each other, whether these are expressed as global citizenship or through some other metaphor.[49] Our common need for environmental stability means that an older population is both inevitable and desirable. A secure old age including income maintenance and health and social care can be achieved only within a framework of social solidarity. Therefore unless social change results in a sense of mutual responsibility across generations which covers all parts of the globe, the twin goals of environmental stability and a secure old age will be unachievable.

5

CONSUMERISM, IDENTITY AND OLD AGE

Liverpool Lass: *When I first married, I lived in a garret in the top of a house in Liverpool 8. As a young man of eighteen, I was more innocent than I thought. In a flat on the landing below, a little grey-haired old lady of about seventy lived on her own. One afternoon, as I came up the stairs, she asked me could I come in to help her. She was dressed in her pink floral housecoat and ushered me into her bedroom. She said her bedside lamp had gone wrong. I sat on the big soft bed with the pink frilly eiderdown and looked at the lamp. I couldn't find anything wrong with it. I tried the bulb, the socket, the switch. I turned to her and said it seemed to be all right. 'Oh, really' she said without surprise, and with a sweet, coy smile which lacked any innocence, made the purpose of the whole charade obvious. As a newly wed, as they say in the* News of the World, *I made my excuses and left. Over the course of the year we lived there, I saw her with a number of different young men, at least one of whom beat her and left her with a black eye.*

OLD AGE AND IDENTITY[1]

The topic of this chapter – that of old age and identity – falls into two parts. These are first, what is the relationship between age *per se* and identity? That is to say, what are the consequences for people's identity of the duration of their life? Are there particular identifiable characteristics which influence the construction of *older* people's identities? The second theme is that of consumption. How do the cultural characteristics of consumer society impact on those whose identity has formed over a long period of time? Are there distinctive experiences of consumption characteristic of older people? These issues will be discussed in the context of debates about postmodernism and its significance for gerontology.[2]

It is suggested that people in the modern social world have more difficulty achieving a fixed sense of identity than people in the past. Knowing who you are and where you fit into society is seen as a problem. This problem is usually understood in terms of 'postmodernity' which forms the starting point for a discussion of the relationship between identity and old age. Postmodern is a term with which it is fashionable to describe the contemporary world: the social and cultural situation at the turn of the century. Some of the features that have been associated with postmodernism are:

- instability, insecurity, flexibility, rapid change, the breakdown of old certainties and social conditions without overarching values or fundamental principles;
- reflexivity, self-awareness, an ability to understand, control and manipulate ourselves and others in unprecedented ways;
- institutional arrangements which reflect these features, including consumerism, fluid family structures, temporary short-term contracts of employment, volatile global markets and identity politics;
- cultural manifestations of these features giving dominance to display, irony, multiple/ambiguous meanings and appearance rather than essence.

To what extent should this view of postmodern culture and society change our view of life in old age? What does old age do to identity maintenance – knowing who we are and getting others to recognise it? Does modern consumer society change the way this can be achieved?

The arguments that there is a special 'postmodern' condition contrast it to the 'modern' world, and similar terms such as 'late' or 'high' modernity are sometimes used to downplay the extent to which the changes represent a radical break with the past. It is suggested that identity is no longer formed by primary socialisation into a culture and such identities no longer form the basis of social integration. The age-based sequences of roles we learn to expect as children lose their meaning. Thus while the twentieth century is viewed as having created a distinctive and stable life course with recognisable stages based around the organisation of employment, the period leading up to the new century, it is argued, has thrown this stability into confusion. 'The final two decades of the twentieth century have seen this confusion accelerate towards a situation where not only are there large numbers of competing cultural messages but also significant expansion in the way that they can be transmitted.'[3] The diversity and uncertainty about the roles we play in society is compounded by the enormously enhanced ability of the media to communicate and display different ways to be old or not to be old. Gilleard and Higgs argue that there is a 'multiplicity of sources that provide the texts and shape the practices by which older people are expected to construct their lives'.[4] This postmodern society without traditional roles or values has a consumer-led culture. Postmodern cultural diversity derives from the cultural abundance available through the marketplace and the media. Featherstone and Wernick identify a commercial culture developing in response to an increasing number of affluent older people:

> Hence when gerontologists argue for the need for positive images of ageing to combat the old models of decline and disengagement, perhaps they should look around themselves in the everyday life of consumer culture where, for the middle

classes at least, positive ageing is alive and well. Of course positive ageing does not provide the solutions to the problems of deep old age and death; its message is essentially one of denial, keep smiling and carry on consuming.[5]

Clearly cultural practice and financial resources are related. Gilleard and Higgs suggest that complex and diverse sources of income in later life make a cultural difference to attitudes about old age. They suggest that 'instead of having little or no expectations of ageing or assuming it will be incorporated into a mass system of entitlements, the need to plan a post-working life establishes a set of new and very different perspectives'.[6] Thus being a 'pensioner' does not mean what it used to in the past and, in the new flexible postmodern world, if we plan properly, the argument suggests, we could buy into new ways of living. Because we can no longer take for granted who we are, we become more self-aware (both as individuals and as a society) and through that self-awareness seek to control our identity. This is known as reflexivity. For some this postmodern confusion and lack of certainty allied to increased reflexivity constitutes a liberation from the constraints of social expectation. The postmodern inspired shift towards culture in social science is important in so far as it strengthens our understanding of the diversity of ways in which it is possible to grow old. Can we now find new ways of being old? To what extent can we choose our identities in old age?

DIVERSITY IN OLD AGE

There are many ways in which the process of ageing creates social diversity. There are different forms of relationships, different kinds of meaning, different structures of opportunity open to people on the basis of how long they have lived. Ageing in the sense of the passing of time is important to identity creation and maintenance. Simple longevity can be significant – living for a hundred years gives a person an important identity. Very old people are often introduced to strangers or introduce themselves in ways which refer to their age. Further, our reputation, as far as it is known, is a key social characteristic derived in part from our past, which determines how we are treated by others. The longer the history of interaction, the greater the chances that social reputations are institutionalised. This can have profound effects on identity. It can, for example, preserve it by insulating identity from current transgressions which may be seen as temporary – out of character. My argument is that although age is vital to identity creation, distinctive aspects of age render such identities unresponsive to 'reflexivity'. This is not to argue for fixity of identity in old age, which is a conceptually and empirically false position. It is to argue that fixity and fluidity are a false dichotomy. Identities have always been more or less malleable by a variety of contingencies. The key point is that in contrast to the postmodern perspective, *old age* identities are not open as matters of personal choice in that they cannot be readily simulated. They cannot be created authentically without the experience of longevity.

Length of life

Old age is defined by time and time should be understood as a social process. Time gives old age an authentic identity that older people can recognise in each other and with which they can cue themselves into a shared place in history. Their fluency in using common knowledge that has been acquired directly through common experience marks them as different from others whose life experience is based in a different time. This is not to deny their free will and suggest that people are simply determined by their experience. People interpret the meaning of their experience differently, and, for example, may try and deny their age and simulate another (usually younger) age. But the fact of the common experience of time means that identity and difference framed around it cannot be an arbitrary creation or a re-creation potentially available to all. Fantasies there may be – fantasies of youth, fantasies of experience – but the genuinely old recognise the authenticity of those such as themselves. It may be possible to be a virgin again in fantasy, but the fantasy and its appreciation depends on not actually being without experience. You cannot simply choose to be old or a member of a particular generation and have others with that identity accept you as authentic. They can tell otherwise. There are three ways in which time impinges on older people. These are duration, age and generation. The experience of time provides an authenticity for each of these elements. It provides a specific type of experience that can be used to legitimise a group identity and demarcate those who share the experience and who are thus different from the 'others' who do not. We can deal with each of these elements in turn.

Duration, the mere passage of time, has implications for old age. Relationships that have lasted forty years have a special character by virtue merely of their duration. There is a symbolic element of 'long-standing' relationships with spouses, or friends, or kin. The 'duration' characteristic of old age identities is the accumulation of life history; having more experience of life simply by having lasted longer is a necessary characteristic of older people. Duration has consequences for identity. Friends, whether or not we see them frequently, are special if they are old friends. Time adds quality to the relationship. A marriage which is fifty years old may be no better or worse than one ten years old, but it is clearly different by virtue of its duration. This observation says nothing about the content of the relationship, good or bad; rather it is to emphasise that time in a relationship has meaning and therefore a range of meanings open only to those who have lived long enough to create them. I would argue that this difference is also something that cannot be simulated, that is not available to the reflexive identity creator except in so far as they can take steps to try to deny or hide it.

Age in terms of social age – the experience of a succession of stages – is different from simply duration. It implies a social career, in work, in family relationships, in life in general. It relates to the issues discussed in Chapter 1 about the normative expectations of the life course. Age in this sense is the appropriate sequence of stages; it does not matter how long the stages are, merely that they follow sequentially. For example, being a grandparent depends on first being a parent, but it does not depend on a specific length of time (other than those set by the reproductive cycles of the human species). Old people have passed through a set of sequences of life-course stages which clearly influence their social and personal identity. Featherstone and Hepworth, writing from a postmodernist perspective, suggest that the life course is becoming destructured.[7] Common social patterns determined by chronological age are becoming less critical to people's life experience. Two key areas where this apparent breakdown of established life-course patterns that have been particularly remarked upon are in the fields of employment and the family. The threefold pattern of school, work and retirement has been undermined. It is suggested that not only is the age of retirement declining, but that there is a whole loosening of the life-course grid. Decreasing labour market stability and rapidly changing employment patterns introduce increased uncertainty and decreased standardisation of the work career components of the life course. Patterns of married life and cohabitation are changing. Divorce rates have increased substantially. For older people, the development of new grandparental roles on the positive side, new forms of social isolation on the negative side, is associated with changing patterns of family life. However, even if Featherstone and Hepworth are correct in that there is a decreasing standardisation in the sequences of roles followed through the life course, the process of sequential roles remains. Although there may be greater diversity, older people's current identity is patterned by time in the sense that they have aged through a sequence of previous identities. This point relates to the unfolding quality of ageing which is discussed below.

Generations are significant sources of identity, different from both duration and social age. They are also validated by common experience. Generation is a cultural phenomenon; a set of symbols, values and practices which not only endure but unfold as a cohort ages. The generation experience may be the recognition of being a teenager at a particular moment in popular culture and authenticated by knowledge and enthusiasm for the popular music of the time. The occasional extrovert 70-year-old hanging around the nightclubs with the teenagers is a quaint deviant, and cannot 'really' be of that generation. It is not simply popular culture that demarcates generations but also very profound common experience such as war and peace. As has been discussed in Chapter 2, generation is the experience of common historical time. The war generation comprising those who experienced the conflict at first hand and lived though the events of 1939 to 1945 has a set of experiences that marks its members as having something in common. They may disagree about the significance of the experience and highlight different aspects, but to be able to tell of one's experiences in a way that authenticates membership of that generation is not easily simulated. Baby Boomers (the 1960s generation) are becoming old and are reinterpreting the meaning and nature of solidarity of their generation. The older generation can successfully act out being young. What its members are able to do is simulate what it was like when they were young. In the right places it is possible to watch athletic, attractive, stunning 70-year-olds dressed up and dancing the night away in a simulation of their youth fifty years ago. What is not on offer is 70-year-olds dressed as contemporary teenagers clubbing at the latest ear-splitting venue fashionable with the current under-twenties.[8] It is easier to change age group than generation. However, we need to understand the creativity of generational cultures throughout the life course, and not see them as merely a reflection of adolescence. These generational cultures are not static, they are not merely the 'old-fashioned' tastes waiting to die out with the older generation, they are constantly being made and remade.

The unfolding of the years

People's lives follow known and predictable careers, but at the same time individuals make choices, sometimes unusual ones, about their future. In sociological terminology, the unfolding of people's lives contains both structure and agency. The life course is not a pathway or route, a concept that suggests a preplanned or predetermined course. A better formulation would involve metaphors of process – career, trajectory, unfolding, dialectic. The traveller at the start of the journey of life does not know where it will end, but the traveller in old age can in hindsight give an account of how and why they arrived where they did. The unfolding character of the life course, in which earlier choices influence the range of subsequent possible choices, can be illustrated in the sphere of work. Employment-career sequences are more than just normative successions of roles. Being a student and then a lecturer, in most cases, is a necessary but not sufficient precursor to being a professor. For the individual, these life-course sequences are not compartmentalised but add to the unfolding dynamic. Work, family and other career sequences are part of a mutual collision of constraints and choices that are people's experience of life. The connections may be seen by the exercise of the 'sociological imagination'.[9] Residential location and housing options and the sequences of household formation and dissolution are mutually structured. The seaside retirement option is more readily available to those owner-occupiers with a paid-up mortgage than, for example, council tenants, or those who, as the result of late household formation, took the option of buying a mortgage at an older age.

Generations differ from each other not only in aspects of socialisation into values and other cultural traits but also in their career opportunities. Different cohorts have had greater or fewer opportunities for economic success, social mobility, migration, personal security, marriage prospects and family development, and many other features structured by historically changing political economies. These structures have an unfolding dimension that is played out as the generation ages and interacts with other generations (see Chapter 2). There is no starting point to the life course where choice is freely exercised untrammelled by the consequences of previous decisions of oneself or others. To this extent free choice is an illusion.

It is useful to think of identity as a process, not a category. Identity is not a list of attributes. The concept of identity encompasses both agency and structure – the 'lived-in' quality of choice and the ascriptive quality of social labelling – and therefore has to be a process. Identity cannot be understood simply by what it *is*, but by how it came about. For older people, their identity has had an unfolding history. They are not the same people as at the start of their lives but, in an essential sense, neither are they different. The change is not encompassed by listing their traits that have changed or those that have stayed the same. Rather it is the continuity of his or her life history and the interlinked parts of its development which give identity to the person.

IDENTITY AND LIFE HISTORY

The elements of time discussed above are part of the process of ageing, experience of which can be part of the identity of different social groups. Identities derived from old age are part of the diversity of society, and thus to be celebrated. However, they are not something that is ephemeral, transient, characteristic only of postmodern society; age, duration and generation are general social phenomena experienced in all societies. Although it may be argued that the experience of rapid social change will tend to make generation rather than age group more salient for modern identity, even rapid social change is not an exclusively contemporary phenomenon. The past is a resource for creating identity; the most unique feature of older people is their long history which provides material for their life-history accounts – accounts created and structured in ways that make sense of and give validity to their identity.

The primary unique feature of older people is their long history. A long lifetime of experience provides materials for life-history accounts, accounts created and structured in ways to make sense of and give validity to identity. When older people give an account of their lives – tell stories to nosy sociologists, oral historians or inquisitive grandchildren – their accounts are based in memory and experience. They recount both a life-course narrative, a sequence of recognised normative progressions from child to adult, from school to work and so on, and also a historical experience: living through the Second World War or going to a live Beatles concert. Long-term historical sociological understanding of changes in the life course and their historical impact depend on historical records of various kinds. But the past is constantly being updated and reinterpreted, as it is a resource for creating identity in the present. Stories about ourselves, as individuals or social groups, are constructed and told in ways that shape our identity. Duration of identity and its unfolding is, for both biographical and group identities, a vital ingredient in establishing a sense of permanence and reality.

Boden and Bielby have studied the significance of the life story or personal narrative in the everyday lives of elderly people.[10] They drew upon a small sample of recordings of conversations between pairs of elderly people and compared them with data collected among young adults. They concluded that among old people there is a broad recalling of the past in the context of the present that achieves for them a shared sense of meaning. They also found that this feature of conversations was far less salient among young adults. In the content of conversations and, in particular, in the patterned organisation of conversational topics, Boden and Bielby demonstrate that elderly people differ from their young subjects in their use of personal address terms, autobiographical resources used to achieve identity, reference to geographical origins, and topic selection and elaboration. These researchers also reported that older people were relatively more fluent in their conversations.

> The elderly in conversation accomplish not only the business of everyday conversation but also a recalling of the past in the

> context of the present through the exchange of fundamental biographical information. Such management of past events and personal biography in conversational interaction appears to be a unique feature of elderly talk, a feature which, we could argue, has significant and relevant meaning in the present lives of the participants, The past for the elderly is a part of the present and appears to have almost equal importance in making sense of current ongoing social interaction.[11]

Boden and Bielby's subjects were strangers to each other. They therefore had to refer to a publicly available repertoire of geography and history to find mutual grounds for conversation. Age implies a life history. Their older subjects communicated with great precision not only details of their lives, but also exchanged common beliefs about the value of money, the state of transport, and matters which served to validate the authenticity of their common experience as older people. Interview research by Kaufman with older people confirms how continuity in a life does not arise spontaneously.[12] As with other aspects of social life, it must be achieved. Individuals must actively seek continuity as they conduct their daily lives and interpret the circumstances of their everyday existence in a way that produces a sense of continued personal identity. Kaufman's research subjects demonstrate the active search for continuity as they apply, adapt and reformulate existing themes to new contexts so that a familiar and unified sense of self emerges and is sustained on a daily basis. She suggests that this may well be true of elderly groups in general.

Claims made by groups to an authentic identity are derived from common experience. Pronouncements are frequently made in the form of 'we are a real group, and you would know this had you had the same experiences as us' or 'you don't know what it is really like unless you are a XX'. You can substitute almost any identity from female to Welsh or teenager into the category. These claims to authentic experience are also claims for independence or autonomy by the group. They justify why others should not legislate for them. Those who do not share the same experiences, it is claimed, cannot therefore understand fully or represent the group. Cohort experience, common, lived-through history, can provide authentication of identity. A generation can make a claim to be a group, and a claim to recognition and autonomy by reference to the particular lived common experiences of that generation. Old age embeds historical and biographic identities unavailable to other parts of the life course.

This foregoing analysis of the relationship between age, time and identity may be used as a basis for developing a critique of simplistic accounts of consumption and identity. Distinctive cohorts – generations – have different lifestyles. These differences are not very convincingly explained by fickle consumer choice. They might in general be explained by a growth in consumer capitalism, but as specific cultural phenomena the differences are rather embedded in the past experiences and opportunities of the members of different generations.

CONSUMPTION AND IDENTITY

Consumption is the definitive cultural activity of postmodern society. In 'post-industrial' society the processes leading to cultural fragmentation have made identity and culture into commodities. Things are bought not because of their use value – how efficient or fit for purpose they are – but for their sign value – what they indicate about the owner. Increasingly what marks individuals out is the way they consume rather than any intrinsic quality they may be ascribed with. However, I would disagree with Gilleard and Higgs that this applies as much to age and ageing as it does to any other socialised attribute.[13] In their eyes ageing has become a much more reflexive project; one involving conscious choice between alternatives available to purchase. However, old age has some special characteristics which mean that it is less susceptible to the ephemera of postmodern consumer identities than Gilleard and Higgs would have us believe.

The irony is that culturally dominant consumer capital-ism, with unprecedented technical ability to reproduce and communicate images and messages, portrays youth as a central value and image, yet demographically most people experiencing these newly diverse consumer opportunities are over age 50. The people exploring postmodern society through new roles and creating new lifestyles are (in the large part) those experi-encing old age in an unprecedented form. Much of the emphasis on identity performance centres on consumption of clothes, styles, bodies and music. Home is also a major site of cultural performance and identity creation. Older people's homes can illustrate these issues of consumption and identity. There may be a few older people having their homes remodelled by interior designers in a complete make-over. Most older people's homes express the continuity of their lives. They are full of furniture and nick-nacks accumulated over a lifetime. There are pictures of family, children and grandchildren. If older people have to move into residential care, they are encouraged to take personal items with which to symbolically re-create their home, and thus help avoid the loss of individual identity associated with institutionalisation.

The image of the consumer is the image of an individual; it represents a social isolate meeting with other social isolates within the hypothetical social relationship of the 'free' market. In reality people are not social isolates; they have a culture and a social history and interact in a variety of institutions through which they obtain the things they consume. To use Warde's words, 'people belong to groups that have a collective history of consumption and, thus, do not enter the department store naked.'[14] Warde makes this point as part of a convincing demonstration that stylistic ephemera are a weak basis for membership or solidarity. Many ethnographies and studies of urban life have identified the complex processes that lie beneath group formation. Identification with the group involves more than acquiring a visual style through purchases. Warde suggests that specialized language, affirmation of authenticity through talk and interaction, nonchalant familiarity with a practical culture and shared judgement serve to distinguish members from pretenders.[15]

Although consumption is clearly highly significant for identity formation in the modern world, it is important to recognise that it is not the exclusive basis for social identity.

The postmodern emphasis on flexibility of identity is based around the triumph of consumerism; it fails to understand its limits. Consumerism is based around the isolated individual in the market. Identities based on consumerism similarly are created and made meaningful in an individualist and impersonal arena. Collective identities require not only co-operation in their construction but social cohesion in their continued social performance. Market-based identities may be ephemeral but other identities are not. Key identities are not related to the market at all. Family and kinship identities are examples. It is not possible to authentically simulate having been married for fifty years. Among the list of identities that it is not possible to simulate in a meaningful sense are those associated with death, and this is discussed at greater length in Chapter 6. Consumption is not a good basis for identity post-death. The sociology of death powerfully points to ways in which death is socially constructed. However, what is not on offer is choice; the individual actors are not free to choose an identity 'dead' which is flexible, reflexive and reconstructable. Once dead there are a variety of identities which may be constructed by others, but none by the deceased. Further, consider the identities of the bereaved, those who are widowed, or who have lost a child. These are not identities anybody chooses and are not ones that are possible to simulate with ease or authenticity.[16] The trauma of the bereavement experience creates an unrecreatable authenticity. The undeniable authenticity of the experience is the quality which makes self-support groups of survivors a powerful and potentially useful experience.

Older people's consumption and identity

Theories that we *are* what we consume may have become popular but need to be understood within a generational framework. Older consumers have distinctive characteristics. The ability of people to signal identity and construct recognisable social positions from things they have bought is not independent of their age. The effects, or potential effects, of consumption on age-related identities include the relative affluence or otherwise of older consumers, the structure of merchandising – what is sold to whom and how – and consumer history, both personal and collective.

Older people's consumption is mediated by their resources, by possibilities of access and by the institutional and legal frameworks through which collective consumption is organised. What identity can the older consumer afford? You cannot exercise free will and partake in consumer choice when you have no money. Marketing is directed towards 'effective' demand. In practice, this means what people can be persuaded to spend. What material resources do older consumers bring to the market, compared to other age groups? There is plenty of evidence to show that there is a growing number of old people who are significantly more affluent than was typical a generation ago.[17] However, the fact also remains that, on average, older people have significantly less spending power than most other age groups in society. As a consequence the commercial organisations through which consumption is organised are not likely to prioritise older people as a group unless this is a specific segmented market, either of products directed specifically to older consumers, or of a limited set of affluent older people. This is reflected in restrictions on older people's access to consumption by the physical structure of retailing. Out-of-town supermarkets effectively discriminate against non-car-owners. Not only are older people less likely to drive or to have a car, but the alternative outlets, the corner shops and city-centre stores, are being driven out by competition. Access to information is structured by age – even such communication devices as telephones, faxes and computers have an age-related distribution. Information is vital to consumers in order to make the market work to their advantage. Social groups with limited market information will be at a disadvantage.

State bureaucracies and other regulatory systems limit access to supply of commodities. For example, many drugs are available only by prescription, and the production, sale and purchase of alcohol are each regulated by a legal framework. Age-based regulations structure access to tobacco, subsidised rail and bus travel, and television licences. Further, older consumers' needs, demands or wants can only be changed into effective consumption if someone is willing to supply them. It is legitimate to ask, 'How does what is on offer in the market fit in with older people's preferences?' These questions have been raised in the context of public services, where an increasing emphasis is placed on 'listening to consumer voices'. The same questions may be asked about the whole retail sector; the 'free market' does not guarantee the existence of suppliers. The market can be structured by ageist stereotypes that may prevent older people from requesting commodities, and suppliers believing they can be offered at a profit.

Older people have a consumption history, and self-evidently this is longer than that of others in society. This consumption history is both personal and linked to the cohort experiences of a developing consumer society. These histories are marked by period effects which can be illustrated by the examples of consumer durables and healthcare. The importance of historical experience of consumption of medical services can be linked to generation changes in supply and demand. Those medical services consumed in old age relate to previous life experience, and the specific occupational and other hazards of the twentieth century. Without a mining industry, there will be fewer miners with black lung in the twenty-first century, asbestosis should decline with the elimination of white asbestos from industrial processes, and while Second World War concentration camps have affected the current generation of older Europeans, ethnic cleansing in the Balkans will affect the mental health of many in the next. In terms of supply, the NHS inherited a set of buildings from the previous medical and welfare regimes; hence it had old work-houses and an over-capacity of TB sanatoria. This history has subsequently coloured many decisions taken on healthcare, not least on the kind of accommodation offered to the chronically sick older population who ended up housed in such buildings.

Consumer history has an 'unfolding' quality. What is bought first influences what is bought subsequently. There are at least four ways in which this happens: through style, technology, scale and anticipatory ageing. The first issue is one of style, what 'goes with' what. Thus clothes or furniture depend on ensemble effects and require a congruence of style and colour. Older people have an established stock of such items, which they do not jettison wholesale. In other words their subsequent purchases of style items are strongly influenced by what they already own.

The second process is based on technical, rather than style, ensembles. Domestic technologies are not independent, so that consumer durables, gadgets and all kinds of equipment are judged by compatibility criteria. Some technologies or devices are more adaptable than others. Gadgets which can be plugged into the existing electrical supply, rather than requiring expen-sive rewiring, will tend to be preferred. One consequence of domestic technology is a pattern to the sequence of purchases of consumer durables – microwave after a freezer, dishwasher after a washing machine. These in turn produce age-related patterns of consumption. Further, the growing technical dominance of some companies and their products structures the market. It is now not possible to purchase 'betamax' video recorders and the VHS standard has become used almost exclusively for domestic video recorders. Thus the longer the history of consumption, the more compatibility issues will structure what older people buy. A further, similar process might be described as sequential problem-solving. Initial attempts to deal with a difficulty have consequences for subsequent attempted solutions. An older person with mobility problems is likely acquire a Zimmer frame after a walking stick and before a stair lift. Older people's need to keep warm in winter will affect their demand for home insulation; however, the method chosen will be influenced by both technical compatibility with the house (e.g. flat roofs which preclude loft insulation) and previous attempts to deal with the situation.

Third, some things cost more and last longer than others. There is a lumpiness to people's investment in their domestic circumstances across their life span. The consequences to one's subsequent life course of buying a house or even a car are very different from purchasing a bus ticket or a loaf of bread. Having purchased a house or a car, a host of other subsequent consumption decisions follow, which will be structured by the initial major decision. This of course gives a distinctive quality to the patterns of consumption of older people. For those older people with only a little money, and their savings tied up or already committed, there is little point to long-range purchases. The purchase of a run-down smallholding with the aim of converting it over a succession of seasons for the self-sufficient 'good life' is not one likely to be made by an 80-year-old.

Fourth, there is the issue of anticipatory ageing, such as is implicit in taking residential options for low mobility, living near informal care from family, or setting aside money for a funeral, which make sense only at certain points in the life cycle. The purchase of a new pair of outdoor shoes or an overcoat may well have different symbolic meaning for an older person compared to a younger one. It may well be a highly symbolic statement about identity. This new dress is not a routine purchase as it will outlast me: can I afford it if I am not going to use it? (I am not an extravagant person). Should I go to church in an old dress? (I am a respectable person). People also have a sense of their own finitude – the closeness of the end point of the life course. The proximity of the end of life has consequences for consumption decisions. These are not merely funeral preparations. Such considerations are built into administrative and rationing arrangements, for example, access to house purchase on a mortgage. Significantly, it appears that access to healthcare is rationed by age; expensive operations may not be considered value for money for people of limited life expectancy.

CHOICE, IDENTITY AND OLD AGE

Although old age necessarily creates identity, such identity is not necessarily popular. Very few people wish to embrace or choose the identity 'old'. This is not to say that the manifestations of longevity will be the same for everyone, rather that all older people will have identities marked by their extra longevity. It is clear that elderly people in Britain today have some common identities derived from their shared generational experience. They share some views of the world that are conditioned by their common historical experiences. They will have experienced defining moments in their life course that are key in constructing an identity which is different for those of a younger age. The current generation of older people as a cohort is also part of pre-'postmodern' cultures. The British senior generation is clearly less at ease with the diversity of modern culture than are younger cohorts.[18] The meaning of the signs through which identity is created arises from the interpretive contexts of family, local community, national and global culture. These contexts, of course, change, not least by the impact of consumer society.

The amount of life experience itself has consequences. Older people by the existence of more life experience have more and as a result probably richer and more complex identity materials. Further, in so far as these identity materials are taken from the world of consumption, they will be structured and limited in the ways discussed above. However, identity is not merely and simply about consumption, it remains deeply socially embedded; formed, understood and elaborated through social relationships. Kinship becomes more important in Western society as people grow older. A longer life adds further potential to social relationships. This potential is not merely the numerical possibilities of interacting with a greater number of people. A relationship, simply by its duration, changes; its symbolic meaning alters. The significance of old friends (i.e. a long-standing friendship) is not how frequently they visit, but the extended continuity of mutual commitment that they give.

Gilleard rightly points out the expanded opportunities of those in a constructive 'third age' as significant consumers. But they are the 'seduced' in Bauman's distinction between the seduced and the oppressed.

> It is all to easy for postmodern tolerance to degenerate into the selfishness of the rich and resourceful. Such selfishness is indeed its most immediate and daily manifestation. There seems to be a direct relation between exuberant and expanding freedom of the 'competent consumer' and the remorseless shrinking of the world inhabited by the disqualified one. The postmodern condition has split society into the happy seduced and unhappy oppressed halves – with postmodern mentality celebrated by the first half of the division while adding to the misery of the second. The first half may abandon itself to the carefree celebration only because it has satisfied itself that the misery of the second half is their rightful choice, or at least, a legitimate part of the world's exhilarating diversity.[19]

Those in residential care at the end of their lives fall largely into the oppressed category. They have a highly restricted participation as consumers and as a consequence have limited active choices in creating meaningful identities for themselves. Older people embedded in enduring social relations experience this most clearly. Role-stripping and social isolation which may accompany deep old age is not a source of liberation and does not lead to the possibility of new and meaningful opportunities for self-expression. For those in deep old age, limited means and opportunities curtail choice of identity, as does their limited prospect for longevity. Those with a long personal history and limited future have to create their identity from other sources.

These are often identities with transcendental meaning that outlast the kinds of identities that can be constructed through consumption and thus remain significant beyond death.

6

OLD AGE, SICKNESS, DEATH AND IMMORTALITY

Priestess: *On holiday in Cuba we walk along a narrow back street of two-storey houses towards the docks in Havana. We stop to look through an open door and see that the small front room is a shrine. There is St Lazarus in yellow decorated with crimson, but because this is the Santeria cult he is also the Yoruba God Babaluaye. A large brown woman of about sixty comes out with a broad smile. We experience great friendliness and patient explanations for my poor Spanish. This is her special saint and he heals people. I put a dollar on the plate. Where are you going? I will show you. So we walk off down the street arm in arm with the priestess in her bright yellow dress and headscarf, down to the ferry.*

KNOWLEDGE OF AGEING AND DEATH

Why does our culture view old age so negatively? Part of the answer lies in its association with illness and death. Why should there be that association? Old age as a cultural category is constructed through its boundaries – where it starts and finishes. We have discussed, particularly in Chapter 1, different ways in which the start of old age is identified. However, old age always ends in death. There are systems of classification which divide up old age (for example, into 'young old' and 'old old'), but old age is always the period of life before death. Old age is therefore understood to a significant extent through the anticipation of death, and is constructed in relation to the ways in which death is understood. Modern society is unique in the extent to which death is concentrated in old age, and the meaning of old age is inevitably tied to issues of longevity and the postponement of death.

Knowledge of ageing and death in modern society is culturally rooted in two historical movements. These are, first, the legacy of the Enlightenment, which identifies progress in terms of advances in scientific knowledge and command over nature. This translates into the medicalisation of old age. In the modern world we construct old age as a medical problem to which science will find a solution. We believe science will come to control human ageing. Second, the secularised modern world is highly individualistic and finds ultimate fulfilment in 'being yourself'. The corollary of this is an emphasis on the body as the site of identity. We feel we must look like who we really are. This presents particularly difficult challenges to sustaining a valued sense of self in an ageing body. The cultural dominance of individualism and of medical science structures the possibility of developing a valued and meaningful old age. This chapter is a critique of the effect of these two trends. How do notions of scientific progress and of individualism structure the ways in which we think about old age? The starting point is to consider 'modern' theories of ageing and to understand the relationship between the biological and social aspects of ageing. We can then be in a position to examine the cultural problem of old age as the stage in life which precedes death, a position that condemns it to fear, loathing and avoidance.

AGEING AS THE SUBJECT OF BIOLOGICAL SCIENCE

The vast majority of research effort in terms of finance and personnel directed towards understanding ageing is in the fields of biology and medicine. There is no universally accepted biological theory of ageing. Different disciplines and institutions seek to speculate about, investigate, test, systematise and register scientific knowledge about ageing. There are basically two images that provide metaphors which scientists use to communicate their theoretical approaches to understanding why organisms age. The first is the 'wear and tear' argument, the process of the body wearing out. The second is a kind of biological 'time clock' approach, a mechanism which triggers an ageing process at a certain time in the life cycle. Many of the advances in knowledge of ageing come in association with better understanding of micro-biology and the complex human biochemistry rather than as a feature of the human organism as a whole. The developments in genetics have favoured the 'time clock' position while major advances in cellular ageing may be seen as a kind of 'wear and tear' argument. I will outline each of these at a very basic level in turn.

It is suggested that the duration of the life span is the result of evolutionary pressures, the result of successful adaptation to a particular environmental niche while our species was forming. This adaptation would include an optimum period of survival which enabled successful reproduction of the species. Human life span from this perspective is the genetic inheritance of the evolutionary process that produced us over millions of years of human adaptation. Evolutionary biologists emphasise that natural selection would not weed out deleterious genes that manifest themselves after the completion of the reproductive years. Hence the older people become, the more such genetic-based problems would emerge and thus limit possible increases in longevity. Increasingly the mechanism for ageing from a biological perspective is seen as a feature of genetic inheritance. This suggests that without an ability to manipulate the human genetic inheritance, it would not be possible to generate human longevity beyond a definite limit. Or, put another way, to achieve the goal of increased longevity it would be necessary to find ways of manipulating the genetic inheritance to overcome the evolutionary acquired limits. The spectacular and well-publicised ability to identify, map and manipulate genetic structures has led to widespread speculation that genetically based limitations on longevity could indeed be manipulated away.

The research on the cellular ageing process has concentrated on understanding the role of oxygenation and free radicals in the ability of cells to sustain themselves. One explanation of ageing suggests that 'free radicals' – highly unstable molecular fragments containing the propensity to damage normal cell functioning – accumulate with age due to the standard process of oxidation and also other sources of wear and tear such as radiation. Some have researched the possibility of limiting this process with 'antioxidants'. These ideas lie behind some of the popular beliefs in the ability of various vitamins to inhibit ageing. Other research is based around stimulating the body's natural processes for limiting the damage done by free radicals. An alternative emphasis on cellular ageing concentrates on the processes by which cells replace themselves. Discoveries in the 1950s established that normal cells have a definite limit to their capacity for replication. This phenomenon was conceptualised as 'ageing' at the cellular level. If we could understand how cells 'know' they are old, then perhaps this biological clock could be changed or turned off.[1] Research into cellular ageing is one of the perceived routes to the scientific control of the biology of ageing. The main problem with translating the understanding of cellular ageing to an understanding of the human life course is the absence of a theoretical basis for generalising from the constituent cellular parts to the whole person.

Human biological ageing needs to be understood through the social and environmental contexts in which it takes place. There is considerable variation in human ageing between people and, even within the same individual, organs do not all age at the same rate. Although some slowing down of bodily function in old age seems inevitable, such processes can be controlled or retarded by human intervention. Factors through life, particularly work environments, nutritional regimes and trauma, influence health in later life. People's health and quality of later life can be modified by appropriate behaviour including proper exercise, appropriate nutrition and similar measures to 'prolong active life'. The well-known example is cigarette smoking, but the history of industrial diseases also illustrates the way in which longevity and a healthy old age is tied up with the way we live our lives. Disentangling the biological from the environmental and social is a way to escape from the fatalism about ageing being an inevitable decline. From the point of view of the older person, loss of hearing and loss of sexual drive may be attributed to inevitable depreciation of old age, but they should also be looked at as solvable problems with practical solutions. Deafness is associated with ageing but was more common in men than women as a result of damaging working environments. The potential solutions are hearing aids that work effectively and legislation on health and safety at work. Sexual activity in old age is as much to do with the social availability of partners as with the ageing of the biological apparatus. Practical solutions exist to enable partners to maintain a mutually satisfying relationship and better health.

There are particular patterns of symptom and disease diagnoses associated with old age. Mobility restricting handicaps such as rheumatism, arthritis and angina become more frequent. Frailty, in particular the weakening of bones, makes some older people more susceptible to fractures. Again, although there is a biological framework to understanding mobility problems in old age this should not be dealt with in front of or to the exclusion of other aspects, such as access to cars and other mobility aids, or suitably maintained public thoroughfares which do not pose a risk to pedestrians. In terms of mental capacities, old age is associated with changes in brain function leading, for some, to Alzheimer's disease or other forms of mental illness. The study of the rise of Alzheimer's disease as a diagnostic category by Ann Robertson shows how historically, institutional processes have elaborated the category 'senile' in ways which structure and control elderly people.[2] Most people do not get Alzheimer's.

Although particular health conditions may be associated with old age, older people's health status is as varied as those of younger age groups. Not all old people will experience ill-health – Table 6.1 suggests that less than one-third of those aged 75 or over report that their health has not been good in the past year, conversely two-thirds do not. Is this particular pot one-third full or two-thirds empty?

In the USA in the 1993 National Health Interview Survey 35.4 per cent of those aged 75 or older reported themselves in 'excellent or very good' health while only 10 per cent reported 'poor' health. This compares with 48 per cent and 7.1 per cent respectively for those aged 55 to 64. Indeed this data suggests that family income makes a much bigger impact than age, with 50.5 per cent of those with family income of $20,000 or more

Table 6.1 Self-reported health by age group

Health on the whole in the past 12 months		*55–59*	*60–64*	*65–69*	*70–74*	*75 and over*
Good	No. in sample	535	493	453	357	418
	%	52.4	50.3	48.0	42.2	32.3
Fairly Good	No. in sample	285	316	310	319	515
	%	27.9	32.2	32.8	37.8	39.8
Not good	No. in sample	196	171	180	168	357
	%	19.2	17.4	19.1	19.9	27.6
Total	No. in sample	1021	981	944	845	1293
	% within	100.0	100.0	100.0	100.0	100.0

Source: Office for National Statistics Social Survey Division, *General Household Survey, 1998–1999* (computer file), 2nd edn. Colchester: UK Data Archive, 3 April 2001, SN: 4134. Author's analysis.

reporting 'excellent or good' health and 4.3 per cent 'poor' health. For those in families with incomes under $20,000 the figures are 32.5 per cent and 12.7 per cent respectively.[3]

A long, healthy life is clearly a highly desirable objective. There are many myths of idyllic rural environments where favoured communities live to their full genetic potential. There are reported communities in which people reputedly live regularly to be 100, 120, even 150. They include Vilcabamba, high in the Andes of Ecuador, parts of the Azerbaijan republic in the Caucasus and Hunza in the Pamirs. When I arrived in Bosnia saying I was to study old age it was immediately assumed I was heading for a small Herzegovina community where it was claimed that many people were centenarians. These places tend to be remote places, high in mountains, with small populations (and gene pools) with clean air, good diet, limited risk of water-borne infection and no long-established registration of births. The power of such symbolic places over the imagination is strong. They are romanticised and idealised communities – the perfect environment for the long life. They symbolically say to us that we could live to over a hundred if only we didn't live in our impure urban environments and lived 'natural' lives. Many people live out a version of this romantic myth through retirement migration. In the West many seek the good old age through moving to favoured locations on retirement. These places are not only rural but also resort areas. In Britain our seaside towns have high concentrations of older people for this reason. Migration is easier in the modern world and this retirement migration is Europe-wide, particularly to the shores of the Mediterranean and other favoured and healthy environments. In the USA, for similar reasons, Florida and California are favoured destinations.

It is common for societies to have a view of a past golden age, an ideal Garden of Eden. Ageing and death came to Eden with the fruit of the tree of knowledge. The Garden of Eden had no sin and no illness. Historically there was a strong association between the two. Hence the secret of long life and good old age was a virtuous Christian life. However, the social logic in practice worked in reverse – as a rationalisation of the current situation. A healthy old person was assumed to have God's blessing and thus must have been virtuous. Those who became sick looked at their past lives and sought to discern the sin which was the cause of their current suffering. This approach to illness is widespread in many cultures and naturally leads to both techniques and rituals to promote longevity by tackling the moral error. There have been magic potions reputedly able to extend life for most of recorded history. They are accompanied by beliefs for the need for expiation, spiritual cleansing, repentance or atonement for sins. In the modern world our lives are replete with potions, pills and lifestyle advice on how to postpone death. Lifestyle advice to avoid sickness and live a good long life comes not only from medical practitioners but also from agony aunts, margarine advertisements and New Age consultants; our culture is saturated with such prescriptions.

THE MEDICALISATION OF OLD AGE

It is important to question why we in the contemporary West think about old age predominately in terms of sickness and disability. The dominance of Western scientific medicine has transformed old age from a natural event to a disease. Successful old age is not seen as it was in the eighteenth and nineteenth centuries as the outcome of a moral life but rather as the absence of disease.[4] Professional knowledge and expertise with which to explain and control the status of old age passed from pastor and priest to doctor and geriatrician. This process is usually associated with the social movement that favoured rationality and the control of nature known as the Enlightenment. Old age became an object of scientific and rational knowledge controlled by experts. It cannot be a subjective experience – you are not 'only as old as you feel' – when there is a scientifically trained expert waiting to tell you the basis of your feelings, how false is your optimism, your probability of survival, and which chemical will make it all better. The history of medicine provides an understanding of the way in which scientifically legitimised knowledge came to dominate thinking about old age. Further, it shows how the treatment of old age within a framework of medical knowledge gave doctors an unrivalled social esteem and professional power. The successful claim to have medical knowledge gives some people literally the power of life and death.

Medical institutions have become so powerful that they can redefine when old age finishes and death begins. The power of science as an institution and the ability of medical science to organise the way we think about life and death are illustrated in a paper by Giacomini in which he examines the history of how the current medical definition of death came about.[5] He clearly demonstrates the association between the power of the medical profession, their needs in the face of changing medical technology, and cultural shifts in the way bodies were classified as alive or dead. Giacomini reports on the process in the late 1960s at Harvard University whereby the concept of 'brain death' was legitimised as a method for defining death.

> First the Harvard Ad Hoc Committee was not charged to question whether brain death *ought* to be defined, or *who* should define it, but rather *how best* to define it. This represents a significant shift from earlier interdisciplinary debates where even medical experts publicly questioned whether brain death legitimately existed, and what 'expert' – physician, the citizen, the theologian, the lawyer – had the right to determine its nature. Further, the Committee successfully established that brain death had standard 'objective', clinical features. The question became not, what 'means' death to family, clergy, caretakers, or to others involved with a patient " . . . " but what 'is' death, in instrumentally measurable terms. The Committee's work succeeded perhaps not so much in institutionalizing specific brain death criteria themselves as in institutionalizing the *practice of medically redefining death* as an historically progressive act.[6]

It may well be argued that just as the latest technology in the 1960s, which was then heart transplants and electroencephalography measuring brain activity, played a key role in this redefinition of death, so genetic technology dominates thinking about old age and death at the start of the twenty-first century. Genetic technology and genetic manipulation are seen as routes to the control of mortality by eradicating disease and scientifically controlling death. The process of medicalisation means old age ceases to be a status within society; it becomes primarily a process of *physical* decline because that is what can be scientifically studied and to which solutions may be found. The human being is dissected into component parts: heart, lungs, limbs, joints, brains and so on. Each is examined, and cures for failures researched scientifically and added to the arsenal of the warriors against old age in white coats. Our belief in the progressive nature of science is such that we are confident that these warriors will ultimately triumph in the final battle with death.

Medical and commercial interests

Elderly people are stereotyped as having disabilities and share with disabled people in general the disadvantages of a negative image. Both elderly and young people experience their physical characteristics as abilities or disabilities in significant measure because of the nature of our society. Both economic and knowledge-based institutions play a role in this. Carroll Estes and her colleagues in the USA and Phillipson and Walker in the UK have pointed out the ways in which dominant professional groups, as well as industrial commercial and political power groups, have developed economic interests in this prevalent view of old age.[7, 8] These powerful groups have the power to structure the lives of elderly people in ways which are financially beneficial to themselves and are controlling of and restricting to the lives of older people. Embedded in such accounts are theories of the significance of age and implicit accounts of why we see old age as a medical problem. The medical-engineering model of health and illness is associated with the commodification of health that has shaped modern institutions which deliver health for older people. Estes *et al.* argue that this approach has produced inadequacies in treatment and quality of care, and distorted incentives in the organisation and delivery of healthcare in the USA.[9] The different history of healthcare in Britain and the USA makes generalisation from the historical specificity of Estes' account of the medicalisation of old age somewhat complex. However, there is much to be learned from these studies. What is common to both sides of the Atlantic are the social and cultural trends that are working themselves out in modern Western capitalism, which link economic individualism to the medicalisation and control of old age.

The medicalisation of old age not only holds out the possibility of a cure for old age but is also profitable. Redefining old age in terms of medicalisation assists the spread of markets into new areas of health and social care where they did not exist before. Modern capitalism is organised around the institution of the profit-making corporation and the use of market mechanisms to maximise the accumulation of wealth. The most profitable markets are new markets with little competition and high returns, and the modern age has seen a constant search for new markets. The removal of social regulation to create new markets has become orthodox political dogma. Old age is commodifiable through the invention of new markets. In the financial markets savings and pensions have been a lucrative and expanding opportunity (as discussed in Chapter 4). The medicalisation of old age creates new markets for drugs, treatments and therapies. In the area of personal care, one can set aside for a moment judgements as to whether care provided by a family out of a sense of love or familial duty or care provided in return for cash provides more satisfactory care, and observe that caring for cash creates new markets for profit-seeking entrepreneurs. However, along with the institutions of the market come values and ideologies; ways of thinking and seeing the world. Older people become simultaneously not only less mobile but also a market for walking sticks or wheelchairs.

For all the benefits Western scientific medicine may have brought in terms of knowledge and control of disease, its continuing dominance enables the further development of the medical-industrial complex.[10] The commodification of old age enables large multinational corporations to expand their activities profitably. Drug companies, finance houses and research establishments have become significant and powerful players in the way our society is organised and in particular for the experience of old age. The medical-engineering model of health and illness and its association with the commodification of health has shaped the institutions through which old age is organised. There are potential conflicts between the two processes of medicalisation and commercialisation; professionals deciding what is best for clients on the basis of professional knowledge, or entrepreneurs offering choice of treatments to customers. However, the combined thrust of medicalisation and commercialisation has been to radically redefine old age, largely so that it is seen in terms of potentially curable illness and treatable medical conditions.

The medicalisation and commercialisation of old age raises resources issues for society and defines the ways these become thought about. The immense investments of resources required to support the ageing enterprise and the medical-industrial complex siphon off capital and other resources for which there may be other priorities. They determine solutions to problems they have created. For example, it might be argued that they drain resources away from the achievement of adequate employment and income that are essential to healthy ageing. Market-oriented policies tend to have the effect of bifurcating society and enabling some people to achieve a successful old age and others to fail. Similarly the nurturing of a healthy environment is a basis for a healthy old age for all. For medical-industrial enterprises the environment is a cost factor, pollutants are costless by-products unless state regulation imposes charges. For them the environment is an irrelevance unless costs are involved; a healthy environment is not the prime organisational objective, since in so far as it prevents ill-health it limits opportunities for profit.

Estes *et al.* argue that 'old age' and 'health' have come to be constructed ideologically as a legitimating rationale that underpins public policy. She suggests three consequences of the medicalisation of old age:

1. Aging tends to be characterized as a process of biological and physiological decline and decay;
2. Some elderly are seen as deserving, while others are seen as undeserving; and
3. Old people and old age are seen as a problem to society. This problem is seen as both special and different and so one of crisis proportions. In this context, care for the elderly is seen to be a major contributing factor to the health care crisis said to be occurring.[11]

The differentiation of medical treatment for elderly people from that provided for other sections of the population is not simply a factor of the prevalence of disease, but of the cultural expectations of old age.[12] Estes *et al.* argue that there are ideological distortions which arise that enable the costs so generated to be used to blame the elderly for causing a crisis – 'for living too long, for using too many health services for not working long enough and for not saving enough.'[13] The medicalisation of old age has become so powerful during the modern period that it may be seen as a form of cultural domination, as a process structuring people's perceptions of old age and thus stifling the possibility of creative cultural activity around old age.

AVOIDING OLD AGE

Biological processes such as birth, maturation and ageing require a societal response. Infant socialisation in all societies includes methods by which the socially demanded control of bodily functions is acquired. Similarly, the biological processes of ageing and death require a societal response. Peter Berger makes the point that death is an essential feature of the human condition and that it is one which requires people to develop means of coping with it. To neglect death is to ignore one of the few universal parameters which impinge upon every social system.[14] On one level this is a functional necessity; if society is to continue it has to find ways of replacing those who have died. On a more existential level, societies have to provide explanations of the world which motivate people to live useful lives and give them access to meaningful explanations and courses of action in face of problems and fears such as death. Secularisation and individualism provide the context of the problem of giving a satisfactory meaning to death. In modern society the problems of old age and death are constructed typically as a medical problem with a scientific solution. We can look at the problems this approach creates for establishing a satisfactory old age by examining science as a dominant culture. We can develop a critique of the ways in which ideas about progress as the scientific control of nature and the chronic individualism of Western society combine to devalue old age by distinguishing the 'liberation from old age' from the 'liberation of old age'.

- The first is represented by the achievement of eternal youth, choosing not to grow old.
- The second is achieved through the construction of a meaningful 'third age'.

Liberation from old age can be created in a number of ways. It is possible for increased length of life to be thought of as a delay in reaching, rather than the extension of, old age. However, the permanent delay of death is immortality. In the modern world, longevity and the postponement of death are seen to be within the realm of science. Technical advances, for example, the possibility of genetic modification and other methods for establishing human control of biological ageing, seem to hold this out as a realistic possibility. However, these claims and objectives need close examination. Societies throughout the ages have used cultural methods for achieving these ends. Myths and magic, rituals and secret knowledge have surrounded death and its avoidance. Death is a social construction; and immortality is also a social construction. Deconstructing the fantasies and modern myths of immortality has important consequences for old age. These fantasies get in the way of dealing with old age as it is, and getting on with constructing a meaningful old age.

In the modern world, embedded in the belief in progressive science is the implication that it will provide the solution for death. Scientists claim to have the techniques for increasing longevity, if not exactly now, at least the potential for the future. Scientific medicine acts as if it should have and eventually will find the cure for death. For the medical technician every death represents a failure. The modern world and its dominant scientific modes of accounting and legitimising knowledge have more than their share of the fountain of youth myths. Wondrous and magic potions or procedures would extend life, much as the young Achilles was dipped in the pool of immortality by his mother. Pathways to such immortality always have an Achilles' heel. The literature of the past hundred years is replete with Dr Moreau characters. Immortality, and the defeat of disease and injury are a commonplace of science fiction.[15] These cultural manifestations are from the same mind-set as that which sees the goal of science as the elimination of death.

Death as a technical problem

Modern Western societies organise their response to old age around the concepts of science and medicine. The prime objective is to prevent death. Indeed as death becomes concentrated in old age, so the costs of healthcare become concentrated in old age. Keeping people alive may be costly but death is always a failure. In modern hospitals there is a sense of failure (and the possibility of accusations of negligence) if life is not preserved. An American study by Timmermans takes Sudnow's description of how the presumed social value of patients affected the performance of hospital staff in attempts to revive them.[16, 17] Since that 1960s study healthcare has undergone dramatic changes and Timmermans examines whether the social rationing described by Sudnow is still prevalent. Increased 'rationalisations' – standardisation in the application of technical criteria and medical practice via protocols, a widely accepted resuscitation theory, and legal initiatives to promote resuscitative efforts and protect patient autonomy – were identified as potential reasons why the situation might have changed. The study was based on observation of 112 resuscitative efforts and interviews with forty-two healthcare workers. Timmermans' pessimistic conclusion is that the recent changes in the healthcare system did not weaken but instead fostered social inequality in death and dying. He argues, first, that the cultural evaluation of old age adversely affects the way older people are treated in a medical context, and second, that the domination of medical knowledge limits the possibility of a 'good death'. With respect to the first issue, that of cultural evaluation of the old, Timmermans links older people with the disabled, and says:

> Unfortunately, the attitudes of the emergency staff reflect and perpetuate those of a society generally not equipped culturally or structurally to accept the elderly or people with disabilities as people whose lives are valued and valuable " . . . " The staff has internalized beliefs about the presumed low worth of elderly and disabled people to the extent that more than 80 percent would rather be dead than live with a severe neurological disability. As gatekeepers between life and death, they have the opportunity to execute explicitly the pervasive but more subtle moral code of the wider society . . . medical interventions such as genetic counselling, euthanasia and resuscitative efforts represent the sites of contention in the disability and elderly rights movements.[18]

Timmermans' studies lead him to conclude that the medical-isation of death creates a number of serious problems, including precluding an examination of the possibilities of other ways to die and to bring old age to a close. Aggressive attempts at resuscitation in emergency departments and relationships with the patients' relatives are structured around a belief in the technical omnipotence of medicine. It is necessary to follow procedures that are intrusive and unnecessary in order to demonstrate officially that the patient was 'beyond the help of science'.

> The prolonged resuscitation of anyone – including irreversibly dead people – in our emergency systems perpetuates a far-reaching medicalization of the dying process " . . . " Deceased people are presented more as 'not resuscitated' than as having died a sudden, natural death. The resuscitative motions render death literally invisible " . . . "; the patient and staff are in the resuscitation room while relatives and friends wait in a counselling room. The irony of the resuscitative set-up is that nobody seems to benefit from continuing to resuscitate patients who are irreversibly dead. As some staff members commented, the main benefit of the current configuration is that it takes a little of the abruptness of sudden death away for relatives and friends. I doubt, though, that the 'front' of a resuscitative effort is the best way to prepare people for sudden death. . . . Relatives and friends are separated from the dying process and miss the opportunity to say goodbye when it could really matter to them, that is when there is still a chance that their loved one is listening.[19]

Research by Jane Seymour within a British context points to significant similarities in the management of traumatic death.[20] In particular, comparison of the two studies shows how the medical, bureaucratic and legal frameworks in each country set contexts for death practices. Like Timmermans, Seymour is able to make the link between the practices in hospitals by which medical staff deal with death and the cultural problems caused by the medicalisation of death. The belief in the power of science to solve the specific causes of death in particular patients is a reflection of the dominance of medical institutions to define death and thus old age.

> Intensive care reflects the modern preoccupation with the mastery of disease and the eradication of 'untimely death'. It is the place to which clinicians may refer a patient when that individual stands at the brink of death and is beyond the reach of conventional therapies. Unravelling the nature of complex disease and predicting its outcome is complicated by the lack of previous familiarity between health care staff and the patient, by the unconscious state of the ill person (Muller and Koenig 1988), and by the advanced technical abilities of modern medicine to blur the boundaries between living and dying.[21]

The medical imperative to prevent death and the belief in the inevitability of scientific progress aligns medicine with the goal of immortality. A goal which implicitly devalues old age by turning it into a realm of failure; success being the permanent postponement of death and the fantasy of immortality.

Fantasies of immortality

The logical extension of the location of death and old age as a technical problem to be solved by science leads to particular modern fantasies of immortality. Attempts to create immortality are hardly new. There have been many attempts to defy death by a variety of means in the past. What is new is the *modern* character of these attempts, and what needs seriously to be addressed is the extent to which modern medicine in trying to repeat the fantasy actually detracts from the possibility of a good old age. An examination of previous symbolic modes of creating immortality can provide insights into the extent to which the implicit medical goal of immortality merely repeats more universal fantasies.[22]

Kinship was the original basis of human society, and the ancient continuities of kinship provide a sense of continuity with one's ancestors and descendants. This is, in some sense, immortality. It is a collective immortality; the individual may pass on but the clan, the lineage, the kin group goes on forever. In our highly individualistic culture, this form is not particularly satisfying. Our greatest cultural goals are individual ones and the survival of our group does not feel like immortality to people living in the modern West. The idea of perpetuating oneself forever in memory has greater appeal. Immortality in memory can be constructed through epitaphs that aid and glorify the memory of the deceased. Memorials in stone and graves with names and words, but also photographs and, as technology improves, sound recordings, video, film and computerised records, may be used effectively to perpetuate the memory of an individual. Protestant culture shows more antipathy to such iconic memorials than Catholic tradition and tends to favour the written epitaph. The Pharaohs' pyramids were constructed from their point of view as mechanisms for eternal life. We do not share their beliefs on how to achieve immortality in the afterlife but we retain a memory of them because of their epitaphs. The Soviet Union built mausoleums and still display the embalmed remains of its founding heroes; since they had no souls the atheist state had to preserve their bodies. Artistic achievement immortalises people by attaching them to an enduring work of art. Similarly, political and religious heroes can be immortalised by cultural practices – public holidays, street names – which ensure their names and stories are reproduced for successive generations.

Immortality in the religious mode entails the eternal life of the believer, whether obtained through resurrection or reincarnation. However, spiritual immortality or absorption into some collective soul has limited attractions in the contemporary essentially secular world. Scientific knowledge puts religion on the back burner, not something to be included in scientific knowledge and thus factored into experimental designs, at best a final unknowable ultimate (and therefore basically irrelevant) source for the law of nature which science discovers. The technology of immortality remains a promise which science is yet to fulfil. However, the power of scientific method, with its confident assertion of the power of reason, is one which few are willing to gainsay. The 'New Age' religions have their versions of immortality, and indeed there are many cults which proclaim methods for corporeal immortality. Not only mainstream science, but all kinds of new quasi-scientific religions follow practices which are intended to ensure longevity. For example, Herb Bowie, author of *Why Die? A Beginner's Guide to Living Forever*, provides the answers to frequently asked questions about living forever on his website.

> I tend to think that the 'secret' to living forever is to take advantage of many small, gradual advances. Research has already determined that many of the symptoms of so-called aging are actually the results of a self-fulfilling prophecy: as people get older, they take gradual deterioration for granted, instead of trying to do something about it. Is it any wonder, then, that they do gradually go downhill? . . . I believe that the key is to change our consciousness – to revise our expectations and belief systems. This is the most fundamental change, and the one that will let us take advantage of all the other advances as they become available.[23]

This website shows the same rhetoric, the same sources of authority and the same structure of argument used by the medical profession in their approach to death; what is missing is an experimental and critical examination of empirical evidence. There is no sharp boundary which can be applied in practice to demarcate pseudo-science and falsehood from medical knowledge and the truth. Both emanate from the social dynamics of modernity and are embedded in self-referential knowledge systems. Both undermine the cultural value of old age and thus limit the possibility of developing a meaningful old age. One way that this happens is clearly shown in the above example; ageing becomes the fault of the individual. It is slackers, morally culpable people who do not follow the best practices of healthy living, that will lose out on immortality and die. The message conveyed by those who supply recipes for immortality and longevity, which are based in reflexive individual self-control, is that if you die it is your own fault.

Given the dominance of biological science in understanding old age and death in the modern world, it is not surprising that there is a proliferation of biologically based techniques and quasi-medical methods for seeking immortality. Modern people can seek to ensure the endless survival of their genes not through kinship but rather through the preservation of sperm and genetic material for use in new technologies designed to achieve the genetic continuity of one's biologically coded characteristics. However, the emphasis on the individual in the modern world directs us to seek personal immortality in bodily form, preferably with the preservation of individual consciousness. One of the earliest groups to have taken active steps to achieve bodily immortality are those who freeze corpses in the belief that future scientific progress would find a way to cure the disease which killed them. Despite the absence of current technology for thawing them out and resuscitating them, faith in the progress in science is believed to justify such procedures. The Alcor Life Extension Foundation offers such a service. Its website describes its view of the process and illustrates the connection between medicine and immortality:

> Cryonic suspension is an experimental process whereby patients who can no longer be kept alive by today's medical capabilities are preserved at low temperatures for medical treatment in the future. Although this procedure is not yet reversible, it is based on the expectation that future advances in medical technology and science will be able to cure today's diseases, reverse the effects of aging, and repair any additional injury caused by the suspension process. These superior technologies could then resuscitate suspended patients to enjoy health and youth

indefinitely. This is the discipline known as cryonics. The Alcor Life Extension Foundation has been providing cryonic suspension services to its members since 1972.

Cryonics is best described as experimental medical technology. This label may seem strange at first, since all persons in cryonic suspension have been declared legally dead. Cryonics is not a new way of storing dead bodies. It is a new method of saving lives.

More than 100 individuals have been frozen since the first cryonic suspension in 1967.[24]

Developments in stem-cell research have certainly enhanced hopes for biological immortality. Stem-cell research holds out the possibility of replacing worn-out or failed parts of the body by growing genetically matched replacements to be transplanted as the need arises. More likely and immediately usefully technologies may come from the use of stems cells to replace diseased nerve cells and thus potentially cure Alzheimer's and Parkinson's diseases. However, we need to note that in line with the medical-industrial establishment's priorities for research, such cures take precedence over strategies for prevention. Cloning technology not only offers the prospect of cloning one's favourite pet so that it is replaced by a genetically identical substitute, it also offers the possibility of reproducing oneself. Immortality and perfectibility are close allies, so the magic possibilities of genetic manipulation and cloning hold out the possibility of perfecting the gene bank and endlessly cloning a perfect you.

Olshansky and Carnes do a good job of debunking sensationalist reports – including medical and demographic accounts – of claims to defeat death and prolong life.[25] In their work most elixirs of life which are advertised and fill the pages of the popular press are suitably demolished and likened to age-old myths and legends. Olshansky has commented that 'the hair goes up on the back of my neck' when he hears some scientists contend that life expectancy will commonly reach 150, 200 years or more. He summarises what he sees as a consensus position on the prospects for human longevity as follows:

There are no lifestyle changes, surgical procedures, vitamins, antioxidants, hormones or techniques of genetic engineering available today with the capacity to repeat the gains in life expectancy that were achieved during the 20th century.[26]

Previous chapters, particularly Chapter 3 where I have discussed the demography of ageing, illustrate that exaggerated predictions of life span to be expected in the twenty-first century are misinformed extrapolations from the increase in average life expectancy in the twentieth century. Science and medicine are assumed to have delivered past increases in life expectancy. However, in practice it has been declines in fertility that have driven ageing populations, and life expectancy has increased because babies now survive, not because older people have exceeded their natural span. Expectations of increased longevity are set in the world view of inevitable scientific progress modelled on heroic medicine of dramatic interventions to individual bodies – surgery, drugs and genetic manipulation. In practice, past gains in longevity are to do with increased hygiene, nutrition and public-health measures. A proper view of the possibilities for longevity takes into account the social conditions that underpin all the changes in longevity. Even if science came up with 'cures' for cancer and heart disease in demographic terms this would not have the effect of increasing life expectancy to the fantasy figures of 130 or 150 years. Even if there is some imminent, dramatic breakthrough in genetic manipulation which creates an extended life span (and there are few signs that there will be) it will be available to only a few affluent people in the West and would not form the basis of a general increase in longevity across the world.

INDIVIDUALISM AND SOCIOLOGY OF BODY

The modern West is a highly individualistic culture. This may be linked to the cultural requirements of capitalism for an 'economic individualism' – people acting in their own immediate material self-interest. It may be linked to a longer cultural tradition such as 'English Individualism'.[27] However, this concentration on the individual has a number of consequences, one of which has been to make people's bodies the focus of their sense of self. People manipulate their body through adornment and at extremes through surgical manipulation to achieve an image that they feel represents them. Thus failures to achieve a satisfactory body image result in particularly modern anxieties. Indeed it creates a particular problem for older people to maintain a satisfactory sense of worth through an ageing body. In deep old age and severe bodily decline, with loss of control of movement, of incontinence, such loss can serve to dehumanise people.[28] Giddens suggests that there is a tendency for modern people to see their identity as increasingly associated with their bodies, and that the prospect of death and decay of the body poses specific existential problems.[29] Adjusting to a changing body image in old age is a key feature of modern ageing.

We can develop the argument about the cultural devaluation of old age and the fantasy of immortality through the insights of the sociology of the body applied to the ageing body.[30] Berger sees secularisation of the modern world as limiting the range of meanings that can be associated with death, and thus failing to meet a fundamental human need for confirming and reassuring explanations of the human condition. It is argued that death has become a particular problem because the body has become so important.[31] Death raises particular difficulties for those whose self-identity is centred on the body as an object that is designed, shaped and moulded towards a particular image. People who value themselves because of the way they have been able to manipulate the way they look are threatened with the loss of that valued self with the demise of the body. People obtain self-esteem, seek to avoid anxiety and to display the virtues they cherish through controlling their appearance. Those who, uncharacteristically for the modern West, concentrate their self-esteem on the preservation of their eternal soul, or on making a contribution to our collective knowledge of the cosmos, are likely to experience old age in a different way. They should ostensibly understand their own death (although perhaps not those of others) in less distressing terms.[32]

Our culture of extreme individualism isolates people from collective meaning systems and responses to death. For a society in which individuality is the supreme virtue, 'ashes to ashes, dust to dust' is a message without consolation. Anthony Giddens argues that changes in society, and specifically what he identifies as the condition of 'high modernity', have made the modern individual's confrontation with death especially difficult.[33] He suggests that radical discontinuity of modernity sweeps away the traditional certainties which he associates with pre-modern societies and which he sees as having provided people with a stable sense of self-identity. However, it may be argued that the whole traditional/modern dichotomy is a false construction. It is an inaccurate and simplistic stereotype hung over from primitive evolutionary anthropology that equates native people with the simple life. It denies these native 'others' history and makes naïve assumptions about the unchanging nature of 'primitive' or simple societies which are not borne out by evidence. Situations of chronic uncertainty and anomie have existed in many historical societies and a search for security is not particularly modern. All cultures manifest some form of bodily manipulation, from piercing, scarring and ornamentation to shaving, cleaning and purification. Funeral preparations across cultures are replete with different forms of ritual manipulation of the corpse. In Western society these tend to be cosmetic, designed to imitate the aesthetics of life. In conformity to the cultural imperatives of modern life, morticians seek to retain each person's uniqueness, which is realised by making them look recognisably like the living individual and 'looking their best' even in death. The modern West is far from unique in use of body symbols and manipulation of the corpse in ways designed to relieve the anxieties about identity and continuity.

The individualism of Western culture is expressed through the values of romantic love. These values massively dominate popular culture and indeed cultural performances of all kinds. The way love is embedded in the body can present problems for old age, and links to the theme of immortality. Devotion to one's children and romantic love are about the only values that are seen to be worth dying for. Love is seen as timeless, true love as a kind of immortality since it is viewed as lasting even beyond the grave. 'Running Bear will meet Little White Dove in the happy hunting ground' – sentiments which this and countless other pop songs and popular novels repeat. However, at the level of concrete social relationships people fall in and out of love, and they express love through physical relationships, and use their bodies to fulfil that relationship. This cultural repertoire fits uneasily with the facts of ageing bodies.[34] Their frailty and impermanence present a serious problem for satisfactorily constructing a transcendental meaning to love. Ageing bodies are challenged by the dominant youthful aesthetic, which makes the slim, muscular body shape desirable, while diminutions of strength, stamina and physical attractiveness in ageing bodies disadvantage their possessors as love objects. Manipulations of the body image to conform to youthful standards of eroticism and desirability have their limits. Few can afford plastic surgery and even such drastic interventions have great limitations. The postmodern idea of people reflexively re-creating themselves by manipulating their body images becomes severely constrained by old age. Bodies in old age tend to be hidden from view. Older people internalise the values of society and can come to regard their own bodies with repugnance, although most are merely reconciled to being 'past it'. To the extent that love is considered to be a sexual, sensual bodily feeling – an erotic experience – then it is thought, and very likely is, to be diminished and deprived in old age and obviously disappears with death. To the extent that love is considered as a spiritual, aesthetic, non-corporal essence it can be thought to endure into old age and survive death. People do sometimes remain 'faithful' to dead partners. They even continue to love partners whose appearance and minds have so decayed that they are unrecognisable as their former selves. However, they can only accomplish this through various psychological processes which involve denial of current experience and which accomplish through memory the preservation of the 'reality' of the former person as the cherished object of love.

OLD AGE AND DEATH

Old age and death are both social constructions. The above discussion indicates how culturally dominant ideas about the medicalisation of old age and about cultural individualism and the body influence the meanings that can be given to death. However, cultural understandings of death are fundamental to establishing the meaning of old age. Death rituals can tell us a great deal about the way society creates the value of the living and in particular the elderly. In many societies death rituals are used in ways whereby the social relationships between the living can be made explicit and kept in good order. Ritual is used to put the dead or dying in a peaceful and benevolent relationship to the living. Such rituals involve paying debts and making gifts. They also usually involve sharing food, which brings together and heals the community after its loss. In many traditional communities value is given to reconciling all social relations and personal feelings prior to death. Confessing sins, putting relationships right so that the deceased can rest peacefully in the grave is part of the process of dying. It is seen as necessary for preventing ghosts, which are the consequence of bad deaths. Failure at such reconciliation, inappropriately celebrated deaths, people who die alone and unmourned, are likely to kindle bad memories – a guilty conscience – and to ignite fears of the dead. The spirits and ghosts of the dead can create mischief in the world of the living unless properly placated ritually. To the world of science and medicine, which is determinedly secular, such fears are 'irrational'. Thus the needs of a social death are subordinated to the technical requirements of death avoidance. As reported above, the medical-legal protocols are followed in a 'ritualistic' fashion which may satisfy institutional requirements but not the need to reconcile the living with the dead. Thus from one perspective, the near dead, those with one foot in the grave, people in the condition of 'old age', are unwelcome, like ghosts, fearful reminders of our own disquiet at death and the failure of self-will and medical science to provide solutions to death.

Fear of death

A fear of death is extremely common and has been taken by many as a psychological universal. Berger sees a necessary role for 'symbolic universes' to give legitimate meaning to death and thus combat the terrifying threat it represents.[35] This creates particular problems in the modern, secular and anomic world. Fear of death affects the way older people are seen, as old age is a reminder of death. The old, it is argued, are feared, and as a result are shunned and segregated since they are a reminder of mortality.

> These processes of individualization and privatization in the organization of death have important implications for the strength of boundaries between the bodies of the living and the dead. Their cumulative effect is to leave many people uncertain, socially unsupported and vulnerable when it come to dealing with death. Elias (1985) argues that this makes people reluctant to come into contact with the dying. . . . Unable to confront the reality of the demise and death of their own bodies, the self-identities of individuals are often made insecure by the presence of death in other people's bodies. This can result in an increase in the boundaries surrounding the bodies of the living and the dying, and a consequent tendency to shun the dying.[36]

Is it possible for death to form a positive value and thus play a less pernicious role in the stigmatisation of old age? If Elias' lonely destiny for old age is to be overcome, it lies in giving a valued symbolic meaning to death. But the converse is also true: to create a meaningful old age, one well resourced, lived in dignity and experienced as fulfilment, can give meaning to death as a good end rather than one to be feared and avoided.

The prospects for the fourth age, then, are not good. A third age is established where independent older people live fulfilling lives and can challenge ageist stereotypes which seek to restrain older people, precisely because they can exclude the power of medical science to say what is normal and appropriate for them. In the fourth age older people lose control of their bodies to the medical professionals. Life at this stage is circumscribed by the postponement of death. However, medical knowledge is structured around the preservation of life and the avoidance of death, and involves a sense of failure (and the possibility of accusations of negligence) if life is not preserved. The consequences are an inability to think about and aim for a 'good' death. The nearest the cultural domination of medical science, and its objectives of keeping the human machine ticking if at all possible, come to understanding a good death is a painless death. The good death is thought of in bodily terms, not human terms. It is constructed in the right dosage of medication; it is not constructed out of human relationships and symbols that transcend individuals and their bodies. The absence of the idea of a good death inhibits a good old age. It means that there is no point at which old age is satisfactorily finished. In the past there have been stronger versions of the 'good death'. We retain such notions still to some extent. The contrast between the sensational death of Princess Diana and the celebration of the long life of the Queen Mother illustrates the point. It is not a shock when someone dies aged 102, it is when a 'young' princess meets a sudden end in a car crash.

Birth and death

In cultural terms birth and death are mirror images. They are equivalent in constructing a meaning to life (Table 6.2).

A good birth and a good death have many things in common. The characteristics of a good birth might be listed as being:

Table 6.2 Birth and death

	Birth and beginning of life	*Death and end of life*
Culturally important boundaries	Pre-human/human	Human/post-human
Socialising nature	A new baby is human, but newness makes it special – not quite human – requiring much work to socialise it into a person	An old body is special by decay and closeness to death but it has not completely lost its humanity, requiring much work in order to socialise it into a proper death.
Transforming nature	Artificial creation of life	Artificial prolongation of life
Human rights	The rights of the foetus	The rights of the brain-dead body
Contested practices	Abortion	Euthanasia

- timely
- wanted
- fulfilling
- free from complications
- embedded in valued social relationships.

The same list will do for a good death. Clearly the most problematic of these terms is the idea of a 'wanted' death. In terms of birth, 'wanted' is a characteristic of the value of voluntarism and personal control typical of modern society, in common with the technical ability to control conception and the manipulation of pregnancy through medical science to achieve desired outcomes. Women are now free to make personal decisions about conception; this is both a technical accomplishment and a moral judgement. Catholic and Islamic objection to birth control is that conceptions should be under divine control. The mirror with death also works here. The technical ability to delay and control death links with an agenda about personal rights, liberties and morality, to create debates about euthanasia and the 'wanted' death. It says something profound about life to have, in the same sense as a wanted birth, a wanted death. It is the culmination of a fulfilled life, one whose aims and tasks are complete. In contemporary individualistic morality, one in which all desires have been fulfilled; in religious terms (particularly in terms of Hinduism and Protestant religious history), one in which all one's duties have been fulfilled. 'Wanted' in this sense has some parallels with birth, but the baby did not will to be born; it was the parents' desire which created a 'wanted' birth. With death the 'want' must be seen to lie with the actor who is dying; death wished by others is much more problematic. One of the complications of the euthanasia debate is ascertaining the true wishes of suffering people and the extent to which well-motivated 'next of kin' should play a part.

Clearly these issues of a 'good death' relate to issues of understanding the cultures of institutions that deal with death for society. Hospitals, mortuaries, cemeteries and in particular old people's homes and hospices have to deal with death on a routine basis. Hospices, which are institutions explicitly for people known to be dying, have the reputation for being better in organising a 'good' death. They are sites where old age becomes death. How they manage the transition has meaning for both. Hospices often have a powerful religious base and are usually strongly against anything that might be thought of as euthanasia.

Adverse consequences of medical immortality

Cultural explanations of death must be coherent with the meaning attached to old age as the time prior to death. To deprive death of meaning or value is to undermine the meaning and value of old age. Attempts to deny, or hide, death will have deleterious effects on old age. If death is to be hidden and avoided, then so will old age. If death is to be denied by the construction of immortality, then old age will be denied. The progression from birth to death gives life meaning; without death there are no stages, no different phases of life. There are many literary and philosophical warnings about the undesirability of immortality. The Czech dramatist Karel Czapek, in his play *The Makropulos Case*, selects the age of 42 as the age at which his central character is empowered to live on indefinitely, so long as she takes an elixir periodically, an elixir prepared for her by her father, a court physician of the sixteenth century. At the time of the action of the play, Elena Makropulos, also known by many other names, has been 42 years old for 300 years. This artistic creation illustrates how a never-ending life leads to an empty, cold, barren, 'lifeless' existence. The character of Elena M., remaining constant, repeats patterns of relationships, successes, failures and so on to the point of excruciating boredom.[37]

Fantasies of immortality are bad for older people. The pre-occupation of our society with the prevention of death and, in particular, the great investment of time, resources and cultural ingenuity to find ways to live longer and if possible for ever, have consequences for old age. These attitudes:

- postpone action on current problems of old age;
- seek technical solutions to cultural problems;
- waste resources in pursuit of undesirable goals.

The medical profession's and biological science's obsession with immortality inhibits research into death as a natural event and the final stage of the life course as a positive meaningful coda. We tend to be more enthralled with technological strategies for transcending death than techniques to revitalise morality and cement social relationships that accompanied death in other times and other places. The concentration on the perpetual postponement of death prevents thought and research that will assist older people to live a good old age and die a good death. High rates of suicide among older people suggest that many do take matters into their own hands – they actively prepare for and instigate their death. To decide the time and place of one's own death is a more positive approach to life than to seek ever more traumatic and desperate fixes to terminal conditions. This is not to suggest that death, particularly suicide, is always a positive thing; just that is some cases it might be. Older people who are driven by despair to take their own lives when they could have been given grounds for hope and optimism is a tragedy. Choice of the time and manner of one's death could on the other hand enhance the possibility of a dignified and valued old age.

The pursuit of immortality is based in cultures that seek liberation *from* old age. A contrasting positive view of the liberation *of* old age will be the subject of the following and final chapter.

Conclusion: old age and ageism

The vignettes I have used at the start of each chapter are descriptions of real people who have formed part of my life and experience. They collectively fall into many of the stereotyped images of old age which trap us into seeing and thinking about old age in particular ways. The patriarch at the head of his extended family, the homely grandmother, the poverty-stricken pensioner, the 'senile', the sexually active older woman, the spiritual older woman, are all part of the repertoire which constitutes the popular understanding of old age, but which also acts as a constraint on older people and the social roles they can play. The skill of good sociology should be to enable us to go behind the stereotypes and see real people acting out their lives within institutional structures and cultural traditions.

LIBERATION OF OLD AGE

We began this book by asking the question: How do we know how old we are, and thus necessarily, How do we come to know what old age is? Part of that answer lies in the construction of cultural meanings and values. Some of these cultural evaluations harden in ageist stereotypes. Ageism may be seen as merely prejudice, a set of attitudes, or it may be considered in terms of socially structured exclusion, institutionalised barriers to partici-pation in society's benefits. The political-economy perspective identifies processes such as the medicalisation of old age as features of ideology – part of the institutional structures confining and limiting the possibilities of old age. How do and how can older people resist the institutional practices that segregate old age and subject it to dissection, manipulation and control? Is it possible for old age to be a time of liberation rather than a time of constraint and decline?

From the perspective of the ageing body the idea of old age as liberation appears to be a nonsense. We cannot escape the constraints of the ageing body. We might try; people go to enormous lengths to manipulate their bodies and to resist the signs of ageing. However, some aspects of ageing bodies are open to re-interpretation. The mid-life end to female fertility has been the subject of much debate about its social significance and is clearly part of the ageing process. However, although some construct this as decline and loss, it can be experienced by some as a liberation. Freedom from reproductive sex in many societies enables women to take on more senior or masculine roles.[1] Social control of reproduction is closely associated with gender relationships. Gender inequalities vary over the life cycle in many societies. In those societies in which male honour and female sexual shame are closely associated, the older body may be in some sense a liberation.

A much more plausible case may be made that old age can be a liberation from social constraints. In social terms this could mean liberation from constraints of middle age. The social obligations of middle age may become burdensome. In terms of the world of work this would mean the end of wage slavery with retirement, and the opportunities of the third age. However, as was discussed throughout this book, such liberation also depends on solving issues of poverty that still afflict many older people. In terms of the constraints of family life, we have discussed the meaning of the empty-nest phase of life. (Note the negative imagery implicit in the term.) However, for some, no longer having dependent children offers the prospect of an expanded social life and greater affluence. Car stickers proclaiming 'recycled teenager – spending the kids' inheritance' suggest at least the potential for liberation in a post-child-rearing period of life.

One of the exciting prospects for the newly developing period of extended retirement associated with the third age is that it offers the prospect of new forms of social relationship. The baby-boomers, the age group who lived through 1960s as teenagers, experienced that time as one of social change and a freedom to form new kinds of social relationship. In the last part of the twentieth century there has been much greater acceptance of a diversity of lifestyles prompted by social movements such as civil rights, feminism, gay rights and the green movement – some-times referred to as a rainbow coalition. Will that generation also seek liberation from cultural constraints of ageism? There are many ideas for new forms of social relationships and institutional arrangements in old age. Andrew Blaikie raises the possibility that radicalism is a generational not an age phenomenon; people do not necessarily become more conservative as they grow older, and the young are not automatically the radicals.[2] It may be that in future old age will be a time for rebellion and any attempt to change the social order while youth is a period of conformity. Betty Friedan suggests polygamy as a solution to the gender imbalance of older age groups.[3] Groups of women, perhaps with a man, living in various forms of domestic arrangement could provide support, care and physical relationships more effectively than widowhood. For some these possibilities represent a night-mare, for others a challenge.

To what extent is it possible to challenge the 'natural' asso-ciation of old age with illness and decline? The movement known as the third age has sought to confront such assumptions. This social movement has attempted to create a positive image for old age as a period of personal development. It has been responsible for many positive developments such as the University of the Third Age which has taken as its task the matching of the desire for education among the retired with the skill and knowledge of retirees. While they have to some extent been successful in establishing the idea of a new positive stage in life, they have failed to overthrow the dominant image of old age as one of illness and decline. The concept of the third age in some circumstances can be an attempt to prolong youth and not necessarily to create a new attitude to old age as a life stage valuable in its own right.

The label 'third age' implies a 'fourth age' as the final part of the life course. The construction of the third age uses the symbols of personal development available with increased leisure time. It stresses the possibility of an active lifestyle – keeping fit, going swimming or rambling. 'Hang-gliding for the over-seventies' is the epigram colloquially used among social gerontologists to suggest the dangers of over-romanticising the 'third age'. The emphasis on the retention of youthful characteristics and interests may revitalise the image of old age for younger retirees, but at some point older people have to curtail their activities, and, even though it may be relatively short, the period before death features ill-health and disability. Thus to retain the integrity of the idea of the third age, social gerontologists invented the fourth age – namely a further period of life after pre-work, work, post-work – and constitutes a final stage of dependency. Thus, despite many benefits, the third-age formula does not overcome the problem of old age; it merely postpones it. It also raises the spectre of people being blamed for their failure to age properly and not sustain fit and active lifestyles.

The way people think about old age in Western society is problematic. In particular the medicalisation of ageing and death has curtailed other possible routes to understanding old age. In the fourth age older people lose control of their bodies to the medical professionals. Life at this stage is circumscribed by the postponement of death. In Western society, to be old is predominantly to be seen as sick. The concentration on ill-health in old age is not natural; it is not an inevitable process but is the product of the way we organise our society (including how we organise and use knowledge). It may be possible that old people are stereotyped as ill and a burden on the health services because they are the objects of other people's knowledge. It may also be possible that old people are stereotyped as unattractive because they lack property and power. Alternatives might be an old age which is seen as an access route to the spiritual power of the ancestors or as a source of knowledge about our common humanity. Such positive perspectives on old age may be found in some other societies.

What may be gained from the discussion of old age presented in this book that provides optimism for the future? Is there hope for a healthy, dignified, revalued old age, lived in material comfort, within a sustainable environment? I have presented both optimistic and pessimistic scenarios. On the one hand there is the view that when the population time bomb explodes there will be poverty, no pensions, social division and conflict and ecological disaster. On the other hand I hope I have also shown the possibilities of resilience, creativity, transformation and fun in old age and where the obstacles to these might lie. Older people should be seen as repositories of cultural wisdom and expertise, craft skills and local knowledge – things that are valuable to all. However, it is important to avoid romantic stereotypes of old age, since elders can also be repositories of prejudice and ancient animosities as well as the positive side of tradition. Old age is capable of re-evaluation as part of sustaining the diversity of cultures, and local technologies capable of sustaining local environments.

Old age cannot be something which is avoided. It is important to distinguish 'liberation *from* old age' from 'the liberation *of* old age'. The first is represented by the achievement of eternal youth, while the second is achieved through the construction of a meaningful 'third age'. Or, to put it in another way, the first is constructed through ageless identities while the second represents a freedom from the constraints of middle age. The first is an illusion, the second a distinct possibility. One conclusion which people who have read this book with sympathy may come to is that old age is not something that happens to people, it is something that is done to them. The alienation from and rejection of old age which is felt by so many in our society may not be a reaction to biological processes but rather the result of a rejection of the social constraints imposed on older people and an alienation from the cultural prescriptions through which old age is understood. Old age could be a valued time of life but we have problems of thinking about it like that. I hope I have been able to suggest some reasons why we have problems thinking in such terms.

Notes

INTRODUCTION

1 This term is used to contrast the politically, economically and culturally dominant societies of the world – most significantly those in Europe, North America and Australasia – with the rest. The 'West' contrasts variously with the 'East' (or Oriental societies), and the 'South' (or the underdeveloped societies).

1 THE EXPERIENCE OF OLD AGE

1 S. Biggs (1997) 'Choosing not to be old? Mask, bodies and identity management in later life'. *Ageing and Society*, 17: 553–70.

2 cf. Evans-Pritchard's account of Nuer time: Chapter 3 in E.E. Evans-Pritchard (1940) *The Nuer*. Oxford: Oxford University Press, pp. 94–138.

3 Kirk Mann (2001) *Approaching Retirement*. Bristol: Policy Press.

4 M. Kohli (1986) 'The world we forgot: a historical review of the life course', in V.W. Marshall (ed.), *Later Life: The Social Psychology of Aging*. London: Sage, pp. 271–303.

5 See Conrad M. Arensberg (1959) *The Irish Countryman*. Gloucester, MA: Peter Smith, and also C. M. Arensberg and S. T. Kimball (1940) *Family and Community in Ireland*. Gloucester, MA: Peter Smith.

6 Pat Thane (1978) 'The muddled history of retiring at 60 and 65'. *New Society*, 3 August, pp. 234–6; Pat Thane (2000) *Old Age in English*

History: Past Experiences, Present Issues. Oxford: Oxford University Press.

7 This difference is currently being phased out. It will take effect in 2010 with the standardisation of age of retirement at 65 for both sexes. This change formed part of the pension 'reforms' enacted in 1995.

8 J. Macnicol (1998) *The Politics of Retirement in Britain, 1878–1948.* Cambridge: Cambridge University Press.

9 On breaching experiments see Harold Garfinkel (1967, 1984) *Studies in Ethnomethodology.* Cambridge: Polity Press.

10 David A. Karp (2000) 'A decade of reminders: changing age consciousness between fifty and sixty years old', in J.F. Grubium and J.A. Holstein, *Ageing and Everyday Life.* Oxford: Blackwell, pp. 65–86.

11 See John Vincent and Zeljka Mudrovcic (1993) 'Lifestyles and perceptions of elderly people and old age in Bosnia and Hercegovina', in Sara Arber and Maria Evandrou, *Ageing, Independence and the Life Course.* London: Jessica Kingsley, pp. 91–103.

12 P. Thompson, C. Itzen and M. Abendstern (1990) *I Don't Feel Old: The Experience of Later Life.* Oxford: Oxford University Press, p. 109.

13 The dictionary translation of *snaga* is: 'Snaga: 1. Power; strength, energy, force; physical strength, will power, will all one's strength, legal force, to be in ones prime 2. Power; horsepower, capacity (as of pipeline), electrical power 3. Forces; military forces; progressive forces.' V.L. Benson (1980) *Serbo-Croatian–English Dictionary.* Belgrade: Prosveta, p. 580.

14 A. Walker and T. Maltby (1997) *Ageing Europe.* Buckingham: Open University Press, p. 53.

15 See for example, P. Johnson and J. Falkingham (1992) *Ageing and Economic Welfare.* London: Sage; and J. Hills (1996) 'Does Britain have a welfare generation?', in A. Walker (ed.), *The New Generational Contract.* London: UCL Press.

16 Department of Social Security 97/192. *Press Release,* 2 October 1997.

17 Office for National Statistics Social Survey Division (2001) *General Household Survey, 1998–1999* (computer file), 2nd edn. Colchester: UK Data Archive, 3 April, SN: 4134.

18 These figures exclude the 7 per cent of households that contain a mix of pensioners and non-pensioners.

19 See for example, D. Street (1997) 'Apocalyptic demography meets apocalyptic politics: special interests and citizens' rights among elderly people in the US', paper presented to The British Society of Gerontology Conference on Elder Power in the Twenty-first Century, Bristol, 19–21 September 1997; and D. Street and J. Quadagno (1993) 'The state and

the elderly and the intergenerational contract: towards a new political economy of aging', in K.W. Schaie and W.A. Achenbaum (eds), *Societal Impact on Aging: Historical Perspectives*. New York: Springer, pp. 130–50. See also C.L. Estes, K. Linkins and E. Binney (1996) 'The political economy of aging', in R. Binstock and L. George (eds), *Handbook of Aging and the Sciences*. New York: Academic Press, pp. 346–61.

20 C. Gilleard and P. Higgs (2000) *Cultures of Ageing*. Harlow: Prentice Hall, p. 23

21 S. de Beauvoir (1972) *Old Age*. London: Andre Deutsch and Weidenfeld & Nicolson; B. Friedan (1993) *The Fountain of Age*. London: Vintage; S. Arber and J. Ginn (1995) *Connecting Gender and Ageing*. Buckingham: Open University Press.

22 Barbara Rogers (1980) *The Domestication of Women: Discrimination in Developing Societies*. London: Tavistock Publications; Janet Momsen and Janet Townsend (1987) *Geography of Gender in the Third World*. London: Hutchinson.

23 HelpAge International Website. Available on-line at <http://www.helpage.org/info/index.html>

24 Maria G. Cattell (1997) 'African widows, culture and social change: case studies from Kenya', in Jay Sokolovsky (ed.), *The Cultural Context of Aging*. London: Bergin and Garvey, pp. 71–98.

25 Indira Jai Prakash (1997) 'The status and condition of elderly widows in India', in *Elderly Females in India*, Society for Gerontological Research and HelpAge, India, New Dehli.

26 Deborah Ewing (1999) 'Gender and ageing', in Judith Randel, Tony German and Deborah Ewing (eds), *The Ageing and Development Report: Poverty, Independence and the World's Older People*. London: Earthscan, p. 42.

27 David A. Karp (2000) 'A decade of reminders: changing age consciousness between fifty and sixty years old', in Grubium and Holstein, *Ageing and Everyday Life*, pp. 65–86, p. 74.

28 P. Spencer (1990) 'The riddled course: theories of age and its transformations', in P. Spencer (ed.), *Anthropology and the Riddle of the Sphinx*. London: Routledge, pp. 1–34.

29 Cf. E. Erikson (1963) *Childhood and Society*. New York: Norton.

30 P. Thompson, C. Itzen and M. Abendstern (1990) *I Don't Feel Old: The Experience of Later Life*. Oxford: Oxford University Press.

31 Ibid., p. 250.

32 T. Dragadze (1990) 'The notion of adulthood in Soviet Georgian society', in Spencer (ed.), *Anthropology and the Riddle of the Sphinx*, pp. 89–101.

33 J. Vincent (1987) 'Work and play in an alpine community', in M. Bouquet

and M. Winter (eds), *Who from their Labours Rest?* Aldershot: Avebury, pp. 105–19.

34 Peter Laslett (1989) *A Fresh Map of Life: The Emergence of the Third Age*. London: Weidenfeld & Nicolson.

35 M.W. Riley (1988) 'On the significance of age in sociology', in M.W. Riley (ed.), *Social Structures and Human Lives*. Newbury Park, CA: Sage, pp. 24–45.

2 THE SUCCESSION OF GENERATIONS

1 S.N. Eisenstadt (1956) *From Generation to Generation*. London: Collier-Macmillan.

2 M. O'Donnell (1985) *Age and Generation*. London: Tavistock. p. 7.

3 E. Cummings and W.E. Henry (1961) *Growing Old, The Process of Disengagement*. New York: Basic Books.

4 As indicated on pages 26–31 and 33, popular and academic language is not particularly clear and specific about the referents for terms such as 'generation', 'age group' and 'cohort'. Vern L. Bengston and, W. Andrew Achenbaum (eds) (1993) *The Changing Contract across Generations*. New York: Aldine de Gruyter (pp. 6–12) have a good discussion of these issues. In this book I have used the term 'generation' in the way which Bengston and Achenbaum (p. 11) describe as the 'European tradition' which follows from Mannhiem as 'age cohorts who share some elements of identity or group consciousness because they share some common experience in history, and who become part of social movements based on age'.

5 C. Phillipson, M. Bernard, J. Phillips and J. Ogg (2001) *The Family and Community Life of Older People*. London: Routledge.

6 The studies replicated by the team were: S.H. Sheldon (1948) *The Social Medicine of Old Age*. Oxford: Oxford University Press; P. Townsend (1957) *The Family Life of Old People*. London: Routledge & Kegan Paul; M. Young and P. Willmott (1957) *Family and Kinship in East London*. London: Routledge & Kegan Paul; and P. Willmott and M. Young (1960) *Family and Class in a London Suburb*. London: Routledge & Kegan Paul.

7 Phillipson, *et al*. (2001), op. cit., p. 251.

8 Ibid.

9 Cf. Judith Globerman (2000) 'The unencumbered child: family reputations and responsibilities in the care of relatives with Alzheimer's disease', in Jaber F. Grubium and James A. Holstein, *Aging and Everyday Life*. Oxford: Blackwell, pp. 386–400.

10 Phillipson *et al*. (2001), op. cit.

11 R. Pahl (1998) 'Friendship: the social glue of contemporary society', in J. Franklin, *The Politics of Risk Society*. Cambridge: Polity Press; G. Allan (1996) *Kinship and Friendship in Modern Britain*. Oxford: Oxford University Press.

12 Young and Willmott (1957), op. cit.; and Willmott and Young (1960), op. cit.; M. Young and P. Willmott (1973) *The Symmetrical Family: A Study of Work and Leisure in the London Region*. London: Routledge & Kegan Paul.

13 Phillipson *et al.* (2001), op. cit., p. 256.

14 Stephen Jackson (1998) *Britain's Population*. London: Routledge, pp. 57 and 84.

15 Phillipson *et al.* (2001), op. cit., p. 256.

16 Ibid. p. 245.

17 Townsend (1957), op. cit.

18 Phillipson *et al.* (2001), op. cit., p. 245.

19 J. Vincent, and Zeljka Mudrovcic (1991) 'Ageing populations in the North and South of Europe: Devon and Bosnia'. *International Journal of Comparative Sociology*, 32 (3–4): 261–88.

20 Phillipson *et al.* (2001), op. cit., p. 251.

21 Ibid., p. 254.

22 M.W. Riley (1988) 'On the significance of age in sociology', in M.W. Riley (ed.), *Social Structures and Human Lives*. Newbury Park, CA: Sage, pp. 24–45.

23 Françoise Cribier (1989) 'Changes in life-course and retirement in recent years: the example of two cohorts of Parisians', in Johnson *et al. Workers v. Pensioners*. Centre for Economic Policy Research. Manchester: Manchester University Press, pp. 181–201.

24 Ibid., p. 183.

25 Ibid., p. 186.

26 Ibid., p. 189.

27 Ibid., p. 187.

28 Ibid., p. 196.

29 Jane Pilcher (1998) *Women Of Their Time. Generations, Gender Issues and Feminism*. Aldershot: Ashgate.

30 Dana Rosenfeld (2002) 'The changing of the guard: the impact of social change on the identity work of lesbian and gay elders'. Paper presented to the British Sociological Association Annual Conference, Leicester, 25–7 March 2002.

31 Ibid., p. 30.

32 John A. Vincent, Guy Patterson and Karen Wale (2001) *Politics and Old Age: Older Citizens and Political Processes in Britain*. Basingstoke: Ashgate Publishers.

33 M.W. Riley, R. Abeles and M.S. Teitelbaum (eds) (1983) *Aging from Birth to Death. Vol.2, Sociotemporal Perspectives*. Boulder, CO: Westview Press for the American Association for the Advancement of Science; J. Finch (1989) *Family Obligations and Social Change*. Cambridge: Polity Press.

34 M.W. Riley, A. Foner and J. Waring (1988a) 'A sociology of age', in H.J. Smelser (ed.), *Handbook of Sociology*. Newbury Park, CA: Sage, p. 30.

35 Peter C. Lloyd (1971) *Classes, Crises and Coups*. London: MacGibbon & Kee; Peter C. Lloyd (1966) *The New Elites of Tropical Africa*. Oxford: Oxford University Press.

36 N. Elias (1982) *The Civilising Process*. Oxford: Blackwell.

37 N. Elias (1985) *The Loneliness of the Dying*. Oxford: Blackwell.

38 K. Mannheim (1927) 'The problem of generations', reprinted in M.A. Hardy (ed.) (1997) *Studying Aging and Social Change: Conceptual and Methodological Issues*. London: Sage.

39 Vincent *et al.* (2001), op. cit.

3 GLOBAL CRISES AND OLD AGE

1 Cf. Nicola Yeates (2001) *Globalization and Social Policy*. London: Sage; Ulrich Beck (2001) *What is Globalization?* Oxford: Polity Press; J.A. Scholte (2000) *Globalization: A Critical Introduction*. London: Palgrave; L. Sklair (1995) *The Sociology of the Global System*. London: Prentice Hall; Malcolm Waters (1995) *Globalization*. London: Routledge.

2 Judith Randel, Tony German and Deborah Ewing (eds) (1999) *The Ageing and Development Report: Poverty, Independence and the World's Older People*. London: Earthscan.

3 HelpAge International website. Available on-line at <http://www.helpage.org/info/index.html>.

4 Ulrich Beck (1992) *Risk Society: Towards a New Modernity*, translated by Mark Ritter. London: Sage.

5 Kenneth Blakemore and Margaret Boneham (1994) *Age, Race and Ethnicity: A Comparative Approach*. Buckingham: Open University Press; Kalyani Mehta (1997) 'Cultural scripts and the social integration of older people', *Ageing and Society*, 17: 253–75.

6 Peter Lloyd-Sherlock (1997) *Old Age and Urban Poverty in the Developing World: The Shanty Towns of Buenos Aires*. Basingstoke: Macmillan.

7 Andreas Sagner and Raymond Z. Mtati (1999) 'Politics of pension sharing in urban South Africa', *Ageing and Society*, 19: 393–416.

8 Lloyd-Sherlock, op. cit.; Peter Lloyd-Sherlock (1999) 'Old age, migration and poverty in the shantytowns of Sao Paulo, Brazil', *Journal of Developing Areas*, 32 (4): 491–514.

9 Gail Wilson (2000) *Understanding Old Age: Critical and Global Perspectives*. London: Sage.

10 US Census Bureau. International Data Base. Available on-line at <http://www.census.gov/ipc/www/idbpyr.html>.

11 Phil Mullan (2000) *The Imaginary Timebomb: Why An Ageing Population is not a Social Problem*. London: I.B.Taurus, p. 61.

12 Stephen Jackson (1998) *Britain's Population*. London: Routledge.

13 Anthea Tinker (1997) *Older People in Modern Society* (4th edn). Harlow: Longman, p. 13.

14 Mullan, op. cit., p. 48.

15 John R. Wilmoth (1998) 'The future of human longevity: a demographer's perspective', *Science*, 17 April, 280: 395–7.

16 John A. Vincent, Guy Patterson and Karen Wale (2001) *Politics and Old Age: Older Citizens and Political Processes in Britain*. Basingstoke: Ashgate Publishers, p. 24.

17 Wilmoth, op. cit.

18 Ibid. Wilmoth cites the following in the quotation: 2. Social Security Administration, Social Security Area Population Projections: 1997, *Actuarial Study* No. 112 (Social Security Administration, Office of the Chief Actuary, Washington, DC, 1997). 3. R.D. Lee and L.R. Carter, *J. Am. Stat. Assoc.* 87, 659 (1992). 4. J.R. Wilmoth, in *Health and Mortality Among Elderly Populations*, edited by G. Caselli and A. Lopez Oxford: Oxford University Press, 1996, pp. 266–87.

19 J.E. Fries (1980) 'Aging, natural death and the compression of morbidity', *New England Journal of Medicine*, 303 (3): 130–5.; J.E. Fries and L.M. Crapo (1981) *Vitality and Aging*. San Francisco, CA: Freeman; S. Jay Olshansky and Bruce A. Carnes (2001) *The Quest for Immortality: Science at the Frontiers of Aging*. New York: W.W. Norton & Co.

20 C. Gilleard and P. Higgs (1998) 'The social limits of old age'. Conference paper, British Society of Gerontology Conference on *Ageing: All Our Tomorrows*, 18–20 September. Sheffield; Olshansky and Carnes, op. cit.

21 Olshansky and Carnes, op. cit.

22 Paul Kleyman (2001) 'Scientists debate human life expectancy', *Aging Today*, March to April. American Society on Aging. Available on-line at <http://www.asaging.org/at/at-218/Scientists.html>.

23 Olshansky and Carnes, op. cit.

24 Kleyman, op. cit.

25 UN (2000) *Replacement Migration: Is it a Solution to Declining and*

Ageing Populations? Population Division, Department of Economic and Social Affairs, United Nations Secretariat, 21 March.

26 Wilmoth, op. cit.

4 OLD AGE, EQUITY AND INTERGENERATIONAL CONFLICT?

1 Note that as identified in Chapter 3, the nature and size of the so-called 'baby-boom' generation varies considerably between countries and in particular between Britain and the USA.

2 K. McMorrow and W. Roeger (1999) *The Economic Consequences of Ageing Populations: A Comparison of the EU, US and Japan.* Brussels: European Commission, Directorate General for Economic and Financial Affairs, Economic papers, no. 138.

3 Ibid., p. 65.

4 Ibid., pp. 65–7.

5 Ibid., p. 67.

6 World Bank (1994) *Averting the Old Age Crisis.* Oxford: Oxford University Press.

7 William A. Jackson (1998) *The Political Economy of Population Ageing.* Cheltenham: Edward Elgar, p. 205.

8 Kirk Mann (2001) *Approaching Retirement.* Bristol: Policy Press.

9 Jackson, op. cit., p. 199.

10 Ibid., p. 198.

11 Phil Mullan (2000) *The Imaginary Timebomb: Why an Ageing Population is not a Social Problem.* London: I.B. Taurus p. 74.

12 Ibid., p. 9.

13 Richard Minns (2001) *The Cold War in Welfare.* London: Verso, pp. 66–76.

14 World Bank, op. cit., p. 292.

15 T. Schuller (1986) *Age, Capital and Democracy.* Aldershot: Gower, pp. 25–7; Sara Rix and Paul Fisher (1982) *Retirement-Age Policy: An International Perspective.* Oxford: Pergamon, p. 125n.

16 Gordon L. Clark (2000) *Pension Fund Capitalism.* Oxford: Oxford University Press, p. 17.

17 T.H. Marshall (1992) *Citizenship and Class.* London: Pluto.

18 R. Titmus (1974) *Commitment to Welfare.* London: George Allen & Unwin.

19 Paul Higgs (1995) 'Citizenship and old age: the end of the road?', *Ageing and Society*, 15: 535–50; Paul Higgs (1997) 'Citizenship theory and old age: from social rights to surveillance', in Anne Jamieson, Sarah Harper

and Christina Victor (eds), *Critical approaches to Ageing and Late Life*. Buckingham: Open University Press, pp. 118–37.

20 Richard W. Stevenson (1998) 'Britons govern their own retirements'. *New York Times*, 19 July.

21 John A. Vincent (1996) 'Who's afraid of an ageing population?', *Critical Social Policy*, 47: 3–26; John A. Vincent (1999) *Politics, Power and Old Age*. Buckingham: Open University Press. Phil Mullan; (2000) *The Imaginary Time Bomb: Why an Ageing Population is not a Social Problem*. London: I.B. Tauris.

22 Stevenson, op. cit.

23 Ibid.; John A. Vincent, Guy Patterson and Karen Wale (2001) *Politics and Old Age: Older Citizens and Political Processes in Britain*. Basingstoke: Ashgate Publishers.

24 A. Budd and N. Campbell (1998) 'The roles of the public and private sectors in the UK pension system', in M. Feldstein, *Privatising Social Security*. Chicago: The University of Chicago Press, available at: <http://archive.treasury.gov.uk/pub/html/docs/misc/pensions/html>.

25 Stevenson, op. cit.; cf. somewhat different projections but similar conclusion in David A. Coleman (2000) 'Who's afraid of low support ratios? A UK response to the UN Population Division Report on "Replacement Migration"'. Expert Group Meeting on Policy Responses to Population Ageing and Population Decline, Population Division, Department of Economic and Social Affairs, United Nations Secretariat, New York, 16–18 October. Available on-line at <http://www.un.org/esa/population/publications/popdecline/Coleman.pdf>.

26 Mishra, Ramesh (1999) *Globalization and the Welfare State*. Cheltenham: Edward Elgar.

27 E.F. Isin and P.K. Wood (1999) *Citizenship and Identity*. London: Sage.

28 D. Harvey (1989) *The Condition of Postmodernity: An Inquiry into the Origins of Cultural Change*. Cambridge: Butterworth; F. Jameson (1991) *Postmodernism: Or the Cultural Logic of Late Capitalism*. Durham, NC: Duke University Press.

29 P. Hirst and G. Thompson (1996) *Globalization in Question*. Cambridge: Polity Press; D. Held *et al.* (1999) *Global Transformations*. Cambridge: Polity Press.

30 Minns, op. cit., p. i.

31 P. Myners (2001) *Institutional Investment in the United Kingdom: A Review*. Available on-line at <http://www.hm-treasury.gov.uk/mediastore/otherfiles/31.pdf>, accessed 6 March.

32 Mark W. Griffin (1998) 'A global perspective on pension fund asset

allocation', *Financial Analysts Journal*, March/April, 54 (2): 60–8; McMorrow and Roeger, op. cit.

33 M.N. Carter (2000) 'Capital markets and occupational pensions: opportunities for the United States and Japan', Marshall N. Carter, Chairman and CEO, State Street Corporation. Website <http://www.us-japan.org/boston/carter.htm>.

34 Ibid.

35 S. Arber and C. Attias-Donfut (2000) *The Myth of Generation Conflict*. London: Routledge, p.13

36 R. Disney, P. Johnson and G. Stears (1998) 'Asset wealth and asset decumulation among households in the retirement survey', *Fiscal Studies*, May, 19 (2): 153–74. However, it is important to understand that there are two interlocking processes at work, one the life-course cycle and the other the demography of age cohorts. Either or both will affect the accumulation of pension funds as they mature after 2010.

37 'KPMG's research found that a third (34%) of companies now operate a final salary pension scheme only. 28% operate a defined contribution scheme, while 36% operate both – evidence that change is already well underway as more and more companies close their final salary schemes for future benefits and switch to defined contribution plans. 44% of final salary schemes were already closed to new entrants.' *Business Credit News UK*, 24 February 2002, 6 (8), available at <http://www.creditman.biz/uk/members/uploads/wf240202.htm#bus news>

38 Clark, op. cit.

39 Emile Durkheim (1964) *The Division of Labour in Society*, translated by George Simpson. London: Collier-Macmillan.

40 Clark, op. cit.

41 Yishai Ashlag (1996) 'Israel's pension fund crisis', *IASPS Policy Studies*, 25, September. Jerusalem: The Institute for Advanced Strategic and Political Studies, <http://www.iasps.org.il/ashlag.htm>.

42 Through much of the 1990s the reformed pensions policies of the Argentine government were presented by many in the financial world (including the World Bank) as a model. However, whatever the causes of the IMF's decision to restrict credit to the Argentine government, the consequence has been the seizure of pension fund assets by the government in an attempt to bolster the banking system. It is not clear who are the winners, but the pensioners are definitely the losers.

Argentina's health insurance system for pensioners (the Integral Programme for Medical Assistance) suspended all non-emergency benefits in early November. It has left many of its four million dependants stranded in what the social services ombudsman, Eugenio Semino, has described as 'the genocide of the old, the sick, and the poor'. Private clinics and pharmacies, which are contracted by the programme, have been underpaid by $160,000 (£114,000) this year. They are turning people away, and their doctors, who have not been paid for five months, have gone on strike. Private clinics that depend on programme funds are reduced to trading with each other for basic supplies such as cotton wool or gauze, and disposable syringes, which are in short supply, are being made to last twice as long as normal. 'If this goes on, in another week or so we will be forced to evacuate all the patients and close down the hospital. People will die', said Dr Juan Alvarez at the Sanatorio Metropolitano in central Buenos Aires.

(Sophie Aries (2001), 'Argentina suspends non-emergency health benefits for pensioners' *British Medical Journal* (24 November), 323: 1206.)

43 Leslie Sklair (2001) *The Transnational Capitalist Class*. Oxford: Blackwell.
44 Richard Lee Deaton (1989) *The Political Economy of Pensions: Power, Politics and Social Change in Canada, Britain and the United States*. Vancouver: University of British Columbia Press; Peter F. Drucker (1976) *The Unseen Revolution: How Pension Fund Socialism Came to America*. London: Heinemann.
45 Robin Blackburn (1999) 'The new collectivism: pension reform, grey capitalism and complex socialism', *New Left Review*, 233: 3–66.
46 Deaton, op. cit.
47 Clark, op. cit.
48 The contrast between arguments over immigration and population ageing is striking. Vincent, John A. (1996) 'Who's afraid of an ageing population?', *Critical Social Policy*, 47: 3–26.
49 J. Urry (2000) *Sociology Beyond Societies*. London: Routledge; Sklair, op. cit.

5 CONSUMERISM, IDENTITY AND OLD AGE

1 Some of the ideas in this chapter have been developed from a paper entitled 'Ideas for conceptualising the dynamics of generation: History and culture in the careers of generations' presented to the 2002 British Sociological Association Conference, Leicester, 25–7 March 2002, and an article 'Consumers, identity and old age', *Education and Ageing*, 14 (2): 141–58, 1999.
2 See e.g. M. Featherstone and M. Hepworth (1989) 'Ageing and old age:

reflections on the postmodern life course', in W. Bytheway (ed.) *Becoming and Being Old: Sociological Approaches to Later Life*. London: Sage, pp. 143–57; C. Phillipson (1998) *Reconstructing Old Age: New Agenda in Social Theory and Practice*. London: Sage; and C. Gilleard and P. Higgs (2000) *Cultures of Ageing*. Harlow: Prentice Hall.

3 Gilleard and Higgs, op. cit., p. 24.

4 Ibid., p. 22.

5 M. Featherstone and A. Wernick (1995) *Images of Ageing*. London: Routledge, p. 10.

6 Gilleard and Higgs, op. cit., p. 22.

7 Featherstone and Hepworth, op. cit.

8 My thirty-something daughter while copyediting the text of this book wrote in the margin at this point: 'You are showing your own membership of the 60s generation. You need to avoid that lack of impartiality. Perhaps instead of your loved-up 70-year-old you could use current nostalgia TV e.g. shared enjoyment of the Clangers which is about identity as someone who loved 1973 and primarily based in youth at that age.' These comments illustrate neatly the cultural specificity of generation and that generational identity is more difficult to simulate than that of age group.

9 C.W. Mills (1970) [1959] *The Sociological Imagination*. Harmondsworth: Penguin.

10 Deirdre Boden and Denise Del Vento Bielby (1983) 'The past as resource: conversational analysis of elderly talk', *Human Development*, 26: 308–19.

11 Ibid., p. 313.

12 Sharon R. Kaufman (2000) 'The ageless self' in J. Grubium and J. Holstein (eds) *Ageing and Everyday Life*. Oxford: Blackwell, pp. 104–11.

13 Gilleard and Higgs, op. cit.

14 A. Warde (1994) 'Consumers, identity and belonging: reflections on some theses of Zygmunt Bauman', in R. Keat, N. Whitely and N. Abercrombie (eds) *The Authority of the Consumer*. London: Routledge, pp. 58–74.

15 Ibid., pp. 71–2.

16 Exceptions to this generalisation may come from a few murderous or fraudulent individuals but such extreme cases could be used to illustrate both the socially constructed nature of bereavement and that such choices are not restricted to postmodernity.

17 P. Johnson and J. Falkingham (1992) *Ageing and Economic Welfare*. London: Sage; J. Hills (1996) 'Does Britain have a welfare generation?', in A. Walker (ed.) *The New Generational Contract*. London: UCL Press, pp. 56–80.

18 See John A. Vincent, Guy Paterson and Karen Wale (2000) *Politics and Old Age: Older Citizens and Political Processes in Britain*. Basingstoke: Avebury. See Chapter 9 for a discussion of generational attitudes to sexual orientation, Europe and citizenship.

19 Z. Bauman (1991) *Modernity and Ambivalence*. Cambridge: Polity Press.

6 OLD AGE, SICKNESS, DEATH AND IMMORTALITY

1 L. Hayflick (1997) 'Mortality and immortality at the cellular level. a review', *Biochemistry* (Moscow), 62 (11): 1180–90. Available on-line at < http://puma.protein.bio.msu.su/biokhimiya/contents/v62/full/6211138 0.htm>, accessed March 2001.

2 A. Robertson (1991) 'The politics of Alzheimer's disease: a case study in apocalyptic demography', in M. Minkler and C. Estes (eds) *Critical Perspectives on Aging: The Political and Moral Economy of Growing Old*. New York: Baywood, pp. 135–52.

3 National Health Interview Survey (1993) (Hyattsville, MD: National Center for Health Statistics) reported in C.S. Kart and J.M. Kiney (2001) *The Realities of Aging*. London: Allyn and Bacon, p. 110.

4 T.R. Cole (1992) *The Journey of Life: a Cultural History of Aging in America*. Cambridge: Cambridge University Press.

5 Mita Giacomini (1997) 'Change of heart and change of mind? Technology and the redefinition of death in 1968', *Social Science and Medicine* 44 (10): 1465–82.

6 Ibid., p. 1479.

7 C.L. Estes (1979) *The Aging Enterprise*. San Francisco, CA: Josey-Bass; C.L. Estes, L.E. Gerard, J. Sprague Zones and J.H. Swan (1984) *Political Economy, Health and Aging*. Boston, MA: Little, Brown; C.L. Estes (2001) *Social Policy and Aging: A Critical Perspective*. London: Sage.

8 C. Phillipson (1982) *Capitalism and the Construction of Old Age*. London: Macmillan; C. Phillipson and A. Walker (1986) *Ageing and Social Policy. A Critical Assessment*. Aldershot: Gower.

9 Estes *et al.*, op. cit., p. 18.

10 Estes, op. cit., pp. 167–78.

11 Estes *et al.*, op. cit., p. 96.

12 Age Concern/NOP (2000) *Turning Your Back on Us: Older People and the NHS*. London: Age Concern.

13 Estes, op. cit., p. 97.

14 Peter L. Berger (1969) *The Sacred Canopy: The Social Reality of Religion*. London: Faber.

15 Andrew Blaikie (1999) *Ageing and Popular Culture*. Cambridge: Cambridge University Press; Mike Hepworth (2000) *Stories of Ageing*. Buckingham: Open University Press.

16 Stefan Timmermans (1998) 'Social death as self-fulfilling prophecy: David Sudnow's *Passing On* revisited', *The Sociological Quarterly*, 39(3): 453–72.

17 David Sudnow (1967) *Passing On: The Social Organization of Dying*. London: Prentice-Hall International.

18 Timmermans, op. cit., p. 467.

19 Ibid., p. 468.

20 Jane Elizabeth Seymour (2000) 'Negotiating natural death in intensive care', *Social Science & Medicine*, 21(8): 1241–52.

21 Ibid., p. 1250.

22 See Michael C. Kearl's excellent presentation available on-line at <http://www.trinity.edu/~mkearl/death.html>.

23 'Frequently asked questions (and answers!) about living forever' by Herb Bowie, 12 November 1998. Available on-line at <http://www.powersurgepub.com/faq/faq.html>.

24 See <http://www.alcor.org/AboutCryonics/index.htm>. (downloaded 26 July 2002).

25 S. Jay Olshansky and Bruce A. Carnes (2001) *The Quest for Immortality: Science at the Frontiers of Aging*. New York: W.W. Norton.

26 Reported in Paul Kleyman (2001) 'Scientists debate humain (*sic*.) life expectancy' available on-line at <http://www.asaging.org/at/at-218/Scientists.html>.

27 Alan Macfarlane (1978) *The Origins of English Individualism: The Family, Property and Social Transition*. Oxford: Blackwell.

28 J. Hockey and A. James (1993) *Growing Up and Growing Old: Ageing and Dependency in the Life Course*. London: Sage.

29 A. Giddens (1991) *Modernity and Self Identity*. Oxford: Polity Press.

30 See Chris Shilling (1993) *The Body and Social Theory*. London: Sage, pp. 175–97.

31 For an excellent study of these and associated issues see Elizabeth, Hallam, Jenny Hockey and Glennys Howarth (1999) *Beyond the Body: Death and Social Identity*. London: Routledge.

32 Shilling, op. cit., p. 177.

33 Giddens, op. cit.

34 Shilling, op. cit., pp. 195–6.

35 See Peter Berger and Thomas Luckman (1967) *The Social Construction of Reality*. Harmondsworth: Penguin, pp. 118–19; Peter Berger (1967) *The Sacred Canopy. Elements of a Sociological Theory of Religion*. New York: Doubleday.

36 Ibid., pp. 189–90.

37 Bernard Williams discusses this example at length in 'The Makropulos case; reflections on the tedium of immortality', in B. Williams (1973) *Problems of the Self: Philosophical Papers 1956–1972*. Cambridge: Cambridge University Press.

CONCLUSION: OLD AGE AND AGEISM

1 For one example see C.W. Hart and A.R. Pilling (1960) *The Tiwi of North Australia*. New York: Holt Reinhardt & Winston.

2 A. Blaikie (2002) 'On the rock of ages', *Generations Review* 12 (1): 11–13.

3 B. Friedan (1993) *The Fountain of Age*. London: Vintage Books.

INDEX

Page references for figures and tables are in *italics*; those for notes are
followed by n